After leaving Oxford Michèle Brown worked as a reporter and presenter for television and radio. She now concentrates on writing and is the author of over a dozen books, the most recent being *The New Book of First Names* and *How To Interview and Be Interviewed*. She and Ann O'Connor have collaborated on two books, *Woman Talk – A Woman's Book of Quotes* and *Woman Talk 2*.

Ann O'Connor was born in Manchester and moved to London just before the last war when she worked in and around Fleet Street. She has helped to research numerous books, including those of the late Poet Laureate John Masefield, and now enjoys concentrating on producing work of her own, mainly in current affairs, particularly as they apply to women.

MICHÈLE BROWN and ANN O'CONNOR

Hammer and Tongues

A dictionary of women's wit and humour

GRAFTON BOOKS

A Division of the Collins Publishing Group

LONDON GLASGOW
TORONTO SYDNEY AUCKLAND

Grafton Books
A Division of the Collins Publishing Group
8 Grafton Street, London W1X 3LA

Published by Grafton Books 1988

First published in Great Britain by
J. M. Dent & Sons Ltd 1986

ISBN 0-586-07439-2

Printed and bound in Great Britain by
Collins, Glasgow

Set in Palatino

CONTENTS

INTRODUCTION

'Too much of a good thing can be wonderful,' said Mae West and that would be our answer to anyone who questions the need for a book of humorous quotations exclusively by women. It is indeed remarkable that most existing anthologies, both general and humorous, have an insultingly small proportion of contributions by women. After all, even those who like to belittle women say they talk too much! – and in serious 'discussions' the answer to the cliché question, 'Why are there no great women painters?' is usually the cliché defence that at least a disproportionate number of the best writers have been women.

Although we felt that there was a self-evident gap to be filled by this book we have not brought to it any campaigning spirit, preferring to let the contents speak for themselves. Our aim has been to create a balanced selection of repartee, gentle humour and the type of wit which encapsulates a small nugget of universal wisdom. As Dorothy Parker neatly sums it up, 'Wit has truth in it; wisecracking is simply calisthenics with words.'

Altogether we have collected over one thousand examples of women's wit and humour. Some of them could *only* have come from women, especially those which take a wry, self-parodying look at what have always been seen as fundamental female concerns – child-birth and raising a family. Yet the book's appeal is far wider, with amusing and apposite quotations for the pre-occupations, pretensions and daily concerns of both sexes. Since it is intended as a comprehensive collection we make no apology for including a good representative sample of the classic quotations, even though some of them may already be familiar. These are greatly outnumbered by what we consider will prove to be the classic lines of the future.

We hope you will have as much pleasure dipping into this collection as we have had compiling it, and in anticipation of any criticism of what we have chosen to include or leave out, we would like to add, in the words of the irrepressible Tallulah Bankhead, 'We don't care what they say as long as they talk about us!'

Michèle Brown
Ann O'Connor   March, 1986.

EDITORS' NOTE

For reasons of space, sources for short quotations, aphorisms, epigrams and reported speech are not given in the text but can be found in the full Bibliography at the end of the book.

Sources are given in the main text where they are relevant to the quotation or where longer extracts have been given.

I might repeat to myself a list of quotations
beautiful, from minds profound; if I can
remember any of the damn things.

Dorothy Parker

Whatever you have read I have said is almost
certainly untrue, except if it is funny, in
which case I *definitely* said it.

Tallulah Bankhead

ACTING

TALLULAH BANKHEAD (1902–68; American actress, also known for her outrageous lifestyle)

It is one of the tragic ironies of the theatre that only one man in it can count on steady work – the night watchman.

ETHEL BARRYMORE (1879–1959; American actress)

Miss Barrymore was playing a scene with Charles Cherry, an elderly actor, which was interrupted by a particularly inconsiderate and noisy group of latecomers. When it was no longer possible to make herself heard Miss Barrymore walked downstage and addressed them, saying, '*I* can hear everything quite clearly but Mr Cherry is rather hard of hearing, do you think you could talk a little louder, just for him?'

CAROL BURNETT (b. 1934; American actress and comedienne)
On Burt Reynolds:

I'm in bed with Burt Reynolds most of the time in the play. Oh, I know it's dirty work, but somebody has to do it.

MRS PATRICK CAMPBELL (1865–1940; English actress)

After she had burst out laughing at George Alexander during a performance of *The Masqueraders*, he sent his stage manager to her dressing room:

'Mr Alexander's compliments, and will you please not laugh at him on the stage?'

'My compliments to Mr Alexander,' retorted Mrs Pat, 'and please tell him I never laugh at him until I get home.'

In his book *Distinguished Company* John Gielgud describes a performance with Mrs Campbell of the 1939 production of Isben's *Ghosts*:

At the end of the play Mrs Alving stands aghast, staring at her son as he mutters, 'Mother, give me the sun. The sun! The sun!' In her hands she still holds the box of pills which she does not

dare to give to him. Mrs Campbell had evidently decided
suddenly that she must make the most of this important final
moment. With a wild cry, she flung the pillbox into the footlights
and threw herself across my knees with her entire weight.
'Oswald! Oswald!' she moaned. The armchair (borrowed by Mrs
Campbell herself from a friend, because, as she said, 'the back is
high enough to hide my chins') cracked ominously as she lay
prone across my lap, and as I clutched the arms in desperation for
fear they might disintegrate, she whispered fiercely, 'Keep
down for the call. This play is worse than having a confinement.'

DAME GLADYS COOPER (1888–1971; English actress)

Asked by Dirk Bogarde what she did about the noise of trains
thundering over Hungerford Bridge above her Playhouse
Theatre, she replied, 'Trains, dear? We had them stopped on
matinée days, naturally.'

JUDI DENCH (b. 1934; English actress)

Judi Dench was highly acclaimed for her performance in the
Royal Shakespeare Company's production of the Brecht play
Mother Courage. However, one performance was less than
successful; a wheel fell off the wagon (the main prop), and the
performance could not continue. As the audience began to get
restless Miss Dench came downstage to explain, very
reasonably, 'We can mend everything about this show except the
wheels. Unfortunately we are the RSC, not the RAC.'

SARAH DOUGLAS (b. 1952; English actress)

A film producer told her how 'cruel and evil' she looked in
Superman II, while off-screen she seemed to be such fun. How
did she manage it?
'In England, dear,' she answered, 'we call it acting.'

DAME EDITH EVANS (1888–1976; English actress)

As a young actress I always had a rule. If I didn't understand
anything I always said it as if it were improper.

Dame Edith, who was acting in *Coriolanus* with Olivier, was hurt in a car crash and out of the play for several days. When she returned she found that Olivier was indisposed in his turn and she would have to put in some extra rehearsal with his understudy Albert Finney. Understandably the young actor was rather tentative about appearing with the legendary Dame Edith and very conscious of the fact that she was still rather badly bruised and shaken by her car accident. Solicitously he asked whether there was anything special he should do. She explained to him that he must only pretend to hold her, otherwise she might wince. He then asked if there were any special moves he should make or anything he did which was different from Olivier which he could correct to make life easier.

'Albert,' was her reply, 'move anywhere you like, dear. I'll get my face in somewhere.'

HERMIONE GINGOLD (b. 1897; English actress)

I got all the schooling any actress needs. That is, I learned to write enough to sign contracts.

PATRICIA HAYES (b. ?1910; English actress)

Asked how she managed to portray the part of Edna the Inebriated Woman so convincingly on television, when she herself didn't drink, she replied, 'It's the people who *don't* drink who know what those who *do* act like.'

HEDDA HOPPER (1885–1966; American gossip columnist)
About a Hollywood 'hanger-on':

At one time I thought he wanted to be an actor. He had certain qualifications, including no money and a total lack of responsibility.

ETHEL MERMAN (1908–84; American musical comedy actress)
On Mary Martin:

She's OK, if you like talent.

DOROTHY PARKER (1893–1967; American writer, satirist and humorist)

On Katharine Hepburn:

She ran the whole gamut of emotions from A to B.

Miss Parker was at the dress rehearsal of her play *Close Harmony* and depressed by what she saw. At one point the director, having watched the over-endowed leading lady intently, whispered to Miss Parker, 'Don't you think it would be better if we made her wear a brassière?' 'Good God, no,' replied Miss Parker. 'At least something in the play is moving.'

DAME MARIE TEMPEST (1864–1942; English comedy actress)

Dame Marie was exceptionally fastidious in her appearance, and even used to stand on a white rug once she had changed into her costume. On one occasion a rather emotional young actress, who had been deservedly scolded for unpunctuality and carelessness during a performance, flung herself at Marie Tempest's feet to beg her pardon, but Dame Marie cut her short with a toss of her head and the brusque command, 'Get up! Get up! Have you no respect for your management's clothes?'

MAUD BEERBOHM TREE (1863–1937; English comedy actress, wife of the actor Sir Herbert Beerbohm Tree)

Lady Tree was acting in *The Mask of Virtue*, a comedy in an eighteenth-century setting adapted from the French. At the dress rehearsal Lady Tree, gazing hopefully across the empty stalls, called to the director, 'Mr A., it seems a little dark on the stage in this scene. Could you oblige us with a little more light? I think you may not have realized that my comedic effects in this play are almost wholly grimacial.'

MAE WEST (1892–1980; American, 'world's greatest movie siren')

Virtue has its own reward, but not at the box office. Why should I be good when I'm packin' 'em in because I'm bad?

After a particularly successful Broadway performance:
I want to thank you for your generous applause – and your very heavy breathing.

I do my best acting on the couch.

QUEEN ALEXANDRA (1844–1925; Danish-born wife of King Edward VII)

On the death of her husband, whose notorious infidelities she had accepted with tolerance and understanding:

Now at least I know where he is!

GRACIE ALLEN (1906–64; American comedienne, who usually worked with her husband, George Burns)

My husband will never chase another woman. He's too fine, too decent, too old.

CAROLINE, DUCHESSE DE BERRI (1798–1870; wife of the son of King Charles X of France)

The Duc de Berri was a terrible husband who made no secret of the fact that he was consistently unfaithful to his wife. After his assassination in 1820 nearly two dozen women from Nantes appealed to the Duchess for financial aid, saying they were pregnant by the Duke.

'How long was my husband in Nantes?' she asked.

A week, they told her.

'Ah, well, then it's perfectly feasible,' shrugged the resigned Duchess.

ZSA ZSA GABOR (b. ?1918; Hungarian-born actress; Miss Hungary 1936; seven times married)

Answering viewers' letters on the American TV show 'Bachelor's Haven' Zsa Zsa was posed the following problem: 'My husband is a travelling salesman, but I know he strays even when he is at home. How can I stop him?

Her simple but effective solution – 'Shoot him in the legs.'

ELINOR GLYN (1864–1943; English novelist and Hollywood scriptwriter)

A man would often be the lover of his wife – if he were married to someone else.

TEXAS GUINAN (1878–1933; American nightclub hostess during Prohibition)

A guy who'd cheat on his wife would cheat at cards.

JULIA (39BC–AD14; daughter of the Roman Emperor Augustus)

Julia was renowned for her immoral behaviour, which was so bad her father banished her from Rome. She had five children, and when someone remarked that, surprisingly, they all bore a striking resemblance to their legal father, she explained, 'That is because passengers are never allowed on board until the hold is full.'

LORRIE MOORE (b. 1957; American short-story writer)

On being a mistress (from 'How to Be an Other Woman'):

It is like having a book out from the library. It is like *constantly* having a book out from the library.

DOROTHY PARKER (1893–1967; American writer, satirist and humorist)

On French novelist George Sand, who had affairs with Chopin and Alfred de Musset, among others:

> What time the gifted lady took
> Away from paper, pen, and book,
> She spent in amorous dalliance
> (They do those things so well in France).

HELEN ROWLAND (1875–1950; American writer)

From *Reflections of a Bachelor Girl*:

One man's folly is another man's wife.

MERLE SHAIN (20th c. Canadian writer)

From *Some Men are More Perfect Than Others*:

So mistresses tend to get a steady diet of whipped cream, but no meat and potatoes, and wives often get the reverse, when both would like a bit of each.

MAUD BEERBOHM TREE (1863–1937; English comedy actress, wife of the actor Sir Herbert Beerbohm Tree)

All Herbert's affairs start with a compliment and end with a confinement.

One night, returning late from a party to find her husband, Sir Herbert, supping *tête à tête* with Esmé Percy, an extremely handsome young actor in his company, she peeped in at the door and murmured, 'The port's on the sideboard, Herbert, and remember it's adultery just the same.'

LADY ELIZABETH WOODVILLE (1437–92; English, wife of King Edward IV)

To Edward IV, whom she later married:

My liege, I know I am not good enough to be your Queen, but I am far too good to become your mistress.

AGE

NANCY ASTOR (1879–1964; American-born British politician. First woman to take her seat in the House of Commons)

On reaching her eightieth birthday:

Years ago, I thought old age would be dreadful, because I should not be able to do things I would want to do. Now I find there is nothing I want to do after all.

JANE AUSTEN (1775–1817; English novelist)

In a letter to her sister Cassandra, 6 November 1813:

By the bye, as I must leave off being young, I find many Douceurs in being a sort of Chaperon for I am put on the Sofa near the fire and can drink as much wine as I like.

TALLULAH BANKHEAD (1902–68; American actress, known also for her outrageous lifestyle)

Age, coupled with drink and drugs, had not been kind to

Tallulah, who had been one of the most beautiful women of her generation. When people approached her to ask if she was really *the* Tallulah Bankhead, she would reply ruefully, in her famous husky drawl, 'I'm what's left of her, darling!'

ERMA BOMBECK (b. 1927; American writer and humorist)

As a graduate of the Zsa Zsa Gabor School of Creative Mathematics, I honestly do not know how old I am.

LADY DIANA COOPER (1892–1986; English socialite)

To a photographer who had come to take photographs for a magazine article when Lady Diana was eighty:

Take your pictures now, my dear, I might die at lunch.

When her name was linked with Sir Robert Mayer – he nearly 100, she 86:

My dear, when you are my age you will realize that what you need is the maturer man.

PHYLLIS DILLER (b. 1917; American comedienne)

I don't know how you feel about old age, . . . but in my case I didn't even see it coming. It hit me from the rear.

From *The Joys of Aging, and How to Avoid Them*:

Sex with older men? I say grab it. But if your man has had a heart attack, don't . . . try to jump start his pacemaker . . . whisper, 'This could be your last one, let's make it good.'

ZSA ZSA GABOR (b. ?1918; Hungarian-born actress; Miss Hungary 1936; seven times married)

When asked which of the famous Gabor women was the oldest:

You'll never get her to admit it but actually it's Mama.

JILL GASCOIGNE (b. 1937; English actress)

I'm 48 – when I get up in the morning I find I left my face hanging on the end of the bed.

ERICA JONG (b. 1942; American writer)

Allow me to put the record straight. I am 46 and have been for some years past.

NINON DE LENCLOS (1620–1705; French society beauty and courtesan)

If God had to give a woman wrinkles He might at least have put them on the soles of her feet.

MARY WILSON LITTLE (19th c.; American writer)

The tombstone is about the only thing that can stand upright and lie on its face at the same time.

LYDIA LOPOKOVA (1892–1981; Russian, Diaghilev ballet dancer and wife of economist John Maynard Keynes)

Spending the night very unexpectedly with Vivien Leigh (Lydia thought she had only been invited to dinner), she was offered a toothbrush. She replied, 'Oh, my dear, do not worry. What is the point of cleaning your teeth? You have to lose them some time.'

MARY MARSH

The only time a woman wishes she was a year older is when she is expecting a baby.

JOAN RIVERS (b. 1939; American comedienne)

The worst thing anyone has ever said about me is that I'm 50. Which I am. Oh that bitch. I was so hurt.

Victoria Principal – if I had a dollar for every stitch in her body I'd be a rich woman. I bought her old car. No matter how far you drive it the clock keeps going back to 33,000 miles.

CONNIE STEVENS (b. 1938; American actress and singer)

On the occasion of a dinner to honour veteran comedian George Burns:

I had a marvellous time last night, and who do you think was my date – George Burns. I picked him up right after his nap . . . It was then I discovered George's secret for staying young. He never overextends himself. He wouldn't even whistle for a cab. He figures when he finally gets up a pucker, why waste it on a taxi . . .

DAME REBECCA WEST (1892–1983; English novelist and critic)
In her eighties, describing to a journalist the night before she had the last of her teeth removed:
The condemned teeth ate a hearty meal.

APPEARANCE

DAISY ASHFORD (1881–1972; English writer who wrote between the ages of 4 and 14)
From *The Young Visiters*, a 'novel' written when she was 9 years old:
I shall put some red ruuge [sic] on my face said Ethel because I am very pale owing to the drains in the house.

MARGOT ASQUITH (1864–1945; English 'socialite' and political hostess, wife of Prime Minister Herbert Asquith)
I have no face – only two profiles clapped together.

MARY HUNTER AUSTIN (1868–1934; American suffragette and writer)
When a woman ceases to alter the fashion of her hair, you guess that she has passed the crisis of her experience.

MRS PATRICK CAMPBELL (1865–1940; English actress)
On a leading lady with whom she was acting:
Her eyes are so far apart that you want to take a taxi from one to the other.

BARBARA CARTLAND (b. 1902; English romantic novelist)
A thin woman will get wrinkles sooner than a fat one. So the

choice is, 'Shall I choose face or figure?' My advice has always
been – have a lovely face and sit down.

MARGARET FISHBACK (b. 1904; American poet and
advertising executive)
From *The Lie of the Land:*

> The same old charitable lie
> Repeated as the years scoot by
> Perpetually make a hit . . .
> 'You really haven't changed a bit.'

TEXAS GUINAN (1878–1933; American nightclub hostess
during Prohibition)
Commenting at the outset of one of her many attempts to diet:
I want to get as thin as my first husband's promises.

MARGARET HALSEY (b. 1910; American writer)
He must have had a magnificent build before his stomach went
in for a career of its own.

VIRGINIA CARY HUDSON(1894–1954; American 'prodigy'
who wrote her collection of essays, *O Ye Jigs & Juleps!* when she
was ten)
Personal appearance is looking the best you can for the money.

JEAN KERR (b. 1923; American playwright and essayist)
From *The Snake Has All the Lines:*

I'm tired of all this nonsense about beauty being only skin-deep.
That's deep enough. What do you want – an adorable pancreas?

From *Please Don't Eat The Daisies:*

Years ago when a man began to notice that if he stood up on the
subway he was immediately replaced by *two* people, he figured
he was getting fat.

BELLE LIVINGSTONE (1875–1957; American courtesan and actress, nicknamed The Belle of Bohemia)

Talking of what were considered the erogenous zones in her youth (from *Belle Out of Order*):

Odd how the erotic appeal has swung away from legs; today a smart girl takes her legs for granted and gets herself a good sweater.

ANITA LOOS (1888–1981; American novelist and screenwriter)

From *Gentlemen Prefer Blondes:*

She always believed in the old adage: 'Leave them while you're looking good.'

ANAÏS NIN (1903–77; French writer)

From *Winter of Artifice:*

. . . all elegant women have acquired a technique of weeping which has no . . . fatal effect on the make-up.

EDNA O'BRIEN (b. 1932; Irish writer)

From *Winter's Tales:*

To Crystal, hair was the most important thing on earth. She would never get married because you couldn't wear curlers in bed.

DOROTHY PARKER (1893–1967; American writer, satirist and humorist)

From 'Cousin Larry':

. . . finger nails of so thick and glistening a red that it seemed as if she but recently had completed tearing an ox apart with her naked hands.

From *The Collected Dorothy Parker:*

Through shimmering heat or stabbing wind Mrs Ewing trudged to her hairdresser's; her locks had been so frequently and so drastically brightened and curled that to caress them, one felt, would be rather like running one's fingers through julienne potatoes.

AURELIA POTOR (contemporary American doctor)

Middle-aged rabbits don't have a paunch, they do have their own teeth and they haven't lost their romantic appeal.

JOAN RIVERS (b. 1939; American comedienne)

My best birth control now is to leave the lights on.

HELEN ROWLAND (1875–1950; American writer)

From the day on which she weighs 140, the chief excitement of a woman's life consists in spotting women who are fatter than she is.

LANA TURNER (b. 1920; American film actress)

When she had a broken wrist:

My left hand's only good for hanging diamonds on.

ARTS

SOPHIE ARNOULD (1740–1802; French opera singer)

On hearing that Marie Guirard, a dancer more famous for her love affairs than her art, which consisted mainly of graceful poses, had broken an arm:

Such a shame it wasn't her leg, then it wouldn't have affected her dancing.

NANCY BANKS-SMITH (contemporary English television critic)

In my experience, if you have to keep the lavatory door shut by extending your left leg, it's modern architecture.

CARYL BRAHMS (?1900–82; English comic novelist and scriptwriter)

From *No Bed for Bacon*:

For ten pounds Beaumont and Fletcher will give you any one of a dozen plays – each indistinguishable from the other.

BETTE DAVIS (b. 1908; American film actress)

On Jayne Mansfield, whose bust measurement was well over 40'':

Dramatic art in her opinion is knowing how to fill a sweater.

DAME MARGOT FONTEYN (b. 1919; English ballerina)

When asked if she believed in women's liberation:

Not if it means I have to carry the male dancers instead of them carrying me.

DAME MYRA HESS (1890–1965; English pianist)

Dame Myra was appearing at a concert being conducted by Sir Thomas Beecham, a man noted for his individual style and eccentricity.

'Will you be conducting from memory again tonight, Sir Thomas?' she asked him.

'Naturally,' he replied.

'In that case,' she continued firmly, '*I* am going to use my music.'

BEATRICE KAUFMAN (American, wife of writer George Kaufman)

Mrs Kaufman, who was not greatly interested in classical music, was persuaded to attend a concert at the Carnegie Hall in which the celebrated conductor Stokowski was conducting Bach's B Minor Mass. Held up in the New York rush-hour traffic, Mrs Kaufman tried to hurry the taxi driver, saying, 'Please drive as fast as you can or we'll miss the intermission.'

GYPSY ROSE LEE (1914–70; American striptease artiste)

> To the music of Rimsky-Korsakoff
> I could never take my corset off
> And where are the sailors who would pay
> To see me strip to Massenet?

BEATRICE LILLIE (LADY PEEL) (b. 1898; Canadian-born comedy actress)

From *Every Other Inch a Lady*:

In my experience, anyone can paint if he doesn't have to . . . During my apprentice days I felt encouraged by the advice of Winston Churchill, who used to say, 'Don't be afraid of the canvas.' I have now reached the point where the canvas is afraid of me.

MAUREEN LIPMAN (b. 1946; English actress and writer)

To Jack (my husband), his violin is comfort and relaxation. To his inky wife, it's time to put her head down the waste disposal unit again.

QUEEN MARY (1867–1953; Consort of King George V)

This story was told by Dame Laura Knight, the distinguished English painter:

Queen Mary had made it a custom to have a very private 'Private View' the night before the Royal Academy dinner, when she and her lady-in-waiting would walk in solitary splendour around the whole exhibition. During these visits she liked as many artists as possible to be present and to stand by their paintings. On one such occasion Dame Laura was in position next to her paintings and her husband, Harold, was a little further along the gallery next to *his* paintings. Coming first to Dame Laura's pictures, Her Majesty paused and chatted for several minutes, then moved on and addressed a few words to the next artist. But after looking at Harold Knight's paintings she moved on without comment. As she passed a little further along to talk to someone else, Harold shrugged his shoulders and said to his wife in a loud stage whisper, 'She doesn't like them.' Queen Mary turned mid-sentence and in an equally loud stage whisper shouted, 'She does!!!!' before continuing with her conversation.

LADY MEUX (née Mildred Sturt; b. ?1890; English aristocrat)

To the artist James Whistler, who was renowned for insulting everyone, including his clients:

You keep a civil tongue in that head of yours, Jimmy, or I'll get someone else in to finish the portraits.

HANNAH MORE (1745–1833; English writer and moralist)
In a letter to her sister, dated 1775:
Going to the opera, like getting drunk, is a sin that carries its own punishment with it, and that a very severe one.

GLORIA STEINEM (b. 1934; American feminist writer, and co-founder of *Ms.*)
From *Outrageous Acts and Everyday Rebellions*:
When my sister took her [my grandmother] to visit a neighbour's new and luxurious house, she looked at the vertical stripes of a very abstract painting in the hallway and said, tartly, 'Is that the price code?'

IRENE THOMAS (b. 1920; English writer and broadcaster)
On her experiences when in the operatic chorus (from *The Bandsman's Daughter*):
. . . Operatic heroines would be the despair of those resourceful ladies who write the answers to readers in magazines. I can imagine them being very stern with a certain Cio-Cio-San of Nagasaki . . . 'Don't depend on this American sailor you say you've met, these whirlwind romances are notoriously unreliable, and since you are only fifteen I think you are too young for a permanent relationship . . . Isn't there a good youthclub in Nagasaki?' To Azucena, Spain, 'Oh dear, what an unfortunate little slip-up that was, throwing the wrong baby on to the bonfire like that, but you really must put the past behind you and not brood so much.' And to Mimi, Paris: 'You really *must* see your doctor about that cough.'

MAE WEST (1892–1980); American, 'world's greatest movie siren')
On hearing that an erotic portrait was an Old Master:
Looks more like an old mistress to me.

DAME REBECCA WEST (1892–1983; English novelist and critic)

Dame Rebecca had been with some friends to the Private View of the Royal Academy Exhibition in Piccadilly. Walking the short distance to the Ritz where they were due to have lunch their attention was caught by a group of people staring into a shop window. Going over, they found that the excitement was being caused by a startling window display of fantastically modern jewellery, all of it in strange irregular and angular shapes and all of it made of the palest gold, studded with rubies. Dame Rebecca cast an eye over it and then turned to her friends with the dismissive remark, 'It looks just like an exhibition of do-it-yourself eczema.'

BITCHERY

TALLULAH BANKHEAD (1902–68; American actress, also known for her outrageous lifestyle)

Zelda Fitzgerald, (in) famous for undressing at cocktail parties in the 1920s, said to Tallulah at one such party, 'Oh, dear, my slip is showing.' To which Tallulah, who was not averse to removing her own clothes, replied, 'You mean your 'show' is slipping, don't you, darling?'

SARAH BERNHARDT (1844–1923; French tragedienne)

The abilities of a young actress whom Bernhardt considered over-rated were being discussed. One of her admirers defended her, saying, 'You must admit she has some wonderful moments.'
   'Oh, yes,' Bernhardt agreed, 'but some terrible half-hours.'

CHARMIAN BRENT (British-born wife of Ronald Biggs, convicted for his part in the 1963 Great Train Robbery)

When her husband, who had escaped to Brazil, was claiming protected status under Brazilian law because his girlfriend Ramona was pregnant with their child, she remarked, 'For a pregnant Brazilian girl Ron's a prime catch.'

ROSABELLA BURCH (Nicaraguan mistress of oil billionaire
Paul Getty in the 1950s)

The American oil billionaire Paul Getty kept a 'harem' of his
mistresses at his English stately home, Sutton Place, where they
spent much of the day bickering among themselves and fighting
for his favours. Among the women were Nicaraguan Rosabella
Burch, who liked to be known as 'Lady Burch', and Ursula
d'Abo, sister of the Duke of Rutland. Russell Miller tells the
following anecdote in his book, *The House of Getty:*
Getty did not like cars to be parked in front of the house, and for a
while the ladies amused themselves by driving each other's cars
round to the front of the house and leaving them in prominent
positions, a manoeuvre in which Rosabella excelled. When Lady
Ursula appeared for lunch in a pair of tailored trousers, Rosabella
flashed her green eyes over them and sweetly inquired, 'Been
working on your car again, darling?'

MRS PATRICK CAMPBELL (1865–1940; English actress)
On Tallulah Bankhead, whose style of acting was diametrically
opposed to that of Mrs Pat:

Watching Tallulah on stage is like watching someone skating on
thin ice – everyone wants to be there when it breaks.

GREER GARSON (b. 1908; Anglo-Irish film actress)
To Joan Crawford, receiving applause after the première of
Mildred Pierce in 1945:

Well, none of us should be surprised. After all, my dear, you are a
tradition.

HEDDA HOPPER (1885–1966; American gossip columnist)
On Joan Collins's appearance:

She looks like she combs her hair with an egg beater.

From *Hedda & Louella* by George Eells:

Hedda Hopper and her arch-rival Louella Parsons were at a
Hollywood nightclub with a party of friends. At the climax of the
show, the director had devised a visual treat which consisted of

setting loose a covey of pastel-dyed doves which were to fly to the stage and position themselves strategically upon the bodies of the semi-nude showgirls. For some reason, on this particular night, the birds became frightened and began to circle about in confusion. When Hedda saw a pastel feather drifting through the coloured lights towards one of the tables, she leaped up, hissing, 'Let's get out of here! Those birds are going to shit! And if they do, I hope they hit Louella's bald spot!'

ELSA LANCHESTER (b. 1902; English-born actress)
After her husband Charles Laughton had returned from a gruelling tour (from *Elsa Lanchester Herself*):

Charles, you look very tired – and fifteen years younger.

ALICE ROOSEVELT LONGWORTH (1884–1980; American, daughter of President Theodore Roosevelt; nicknamed 'Princess Malice')
When asked her opinion of journalist Dorothy Thompson:
She is the only woman who had her menopause in public and got paid for it.

Alice had nothing kind to say about politicians. Hearing that the wife of Calvin Coolidge, a man of few words, had once taught at a school for the deaf and dumb, she remarked, 'That made it easier for her to live with Calvin.'

DOROTHY PARKER (1893–1967; American writer, satirist and humorist)
To a fellow-guest as they both gazed at their hostess's battered toothbrush:

I think she rides it on Halloween.

Reviewing Margot Asquith's *Lay Sermons* for the *New Yorker*, 22 October 1927:

The affair between Margot Asquith and Margot Asquith will live as one of the prettiest love stories in all literature.

JOAN RIVERS (b. 1939; American comedienne)

On Jane Fonda (and her husband):

Jane's got a good body. But God gives and God takes away – she's got to sleep with Tom Hayden.

MAE WEST (1892–1980; American, 'world's greatest movie siren')

He's the kind of man who picks his friends – to pieces.

PATRICE WYMORE (b. 1929; American, third wife of Errol Flynn)

On Errol Flynn's intellectual capacity:

Well, you know Daddyo – if he sends a telegram he gets writer's cramp.

CAREERS

POLLY ADLER (1900–62; American, highly successful 'madam', on whom the play *The Greatest Little Whorehouse in Texas* was based)

Too many cooks spoil the brothel.

SUSAN B. ANTHONY (1820–1906; American pioneer feminist and temperance campaigner)

In a speech to a State Convention of Schoolteachers:

Gentlemen, do you not see that so long as society says a woman is incompetent to be a lawyer, minister or doctor, but has ample ability to be a teacher, every man of you who chooses this profession tacitly acknowledges that he has no more brains than a woman?

VICTORIA BILLINGS (b. 1945; American journalist and writer)

The best thing that could happen to motherhood already has. Fewer women are going into it.

BETTE DAVIS (b. 1908; American film actress with a reputation for being hard bitten)

When her career was in the doldrums she placed the following advertisement in *Variety* and *The Hollywood Reporter:*

Situation Wanted

Mother of three (10, 11 and 15). Divorcee. American. Thirty years' experience as an actress in motion pictures. Mobile still and more affable than rumour would have it. Wants steady employment in Hollywood. (Has had Broadway.) Bette Davis. References upon request.

HERMIONE GINGOLD (b. 1897; English actress)

From *The World Is Square:*

My father dealt in stocks and shares and my mother also had a lot of time on her hands.

BILLIE HOLLIDAY (1915–59; American 'blues' singer)

I'm always making a comeback but nobody ever tells me where I've been.

XAVIERA HOLLANDER (b. ?1936; Dutch prostitute, 'The Happy Hooker')

Actually, if my business was legitimate, I would deduct a substantial percentage for depreciation of my body.

PENELOPE KEITH (b. ?1941; English actress)

One of the good things about working in television is that you know where the canteen is and this gives you a great sense of security.

MAUREEN LIPMAN (b. 1946; English actress and writer)

When her teachers and family said she needed some training to fall back on before she took up a stage career:

I'm going to fall back on the casting couch.

BELLE LIVINGSTONE (1875–1957; American courtesan and actress, nicknamed The Belle of Bohemia)

The courtesan, alas, is gone, extinct as the American buffalo . . .
Anyone can become a mistress; one has to be born a courtesan.

SHIRLEY MACLAINE (b. 1934; American dancer and actress)

I've made so many movies playing a hooker that they don't pay me in the regular way any more. They leave it on the dresser.

VIRGINIA OSTMAN

If lawyers are debarred and clergymen defrocked, doesn't it follow that electricians can be delighted; musicians denoted; cowboys deranged; models deposed; tree surgeons debarked and dry cleaners depressed?

DOROTHY PARKER (1893–1967; American writer, satirist and humorist)

On giving up her book column 'Constant Reader' in the *New Yorker*:

I am about to leave literature flat on its face. I don't want to review books any more. It cuts in too much on my reading.

MRS HENRY J. SERWAT

Quoted in *Bartlett's Unfamiliar Quotations*:

Bureaucracy is based on a willingness either to pass the buck or to spend it.

MAE WEST (1892–1980; American, 'world's greatest movie siren')

I always say keep a diary and some day it'll keep you.

CHILDREN

PAM AYRES (contemporary English writer of humorous verse)
    'Foghorn Lullaby'

    Go to sleep my little foghorn
    Give your poor old throat a rest

Of all the little foghorns
You're the one I love the best
You're the dearest little foghorn
In the country or the town
But how I sometimes wish
That I could turn the volume down!

MRS G. BAXTER
Quoted in *Bartlett's Unfamiliar Quotations*:

Out of the mouths of babes – usually when you've got your best suit on.

SARAH BERNHARDT (1844–1923; French tragedienne)
To the actress Madge Kendal, who complained that Sarah Bernhardt's roles were often too 'passionate' for her to bring her daughter to the theatre:

Madame, had it not been for passion you would have no daughter to bring.

ERMA BOMBECK (b. 1927; American writer and humorist)
From *Motherhood: The Second Oldest Profession*:

In general my children refused to eat anything that hadn't danced on TV.

A course on Legal Rights for Mothers (from *Motherhood*):

Know the law. Are you required to transport laundry that has been in the utility room longer than sixty days?

Do you have the right to open a bedroom door with a skewer, or would this be considered illegal entry?

Can you abandon a child along a public highway for kicking Daddy's seat for 600 miles?

Are you liable for desertion if you move and don't tell your grown son where you are going?

A panel of legal experts will discuss how binding is the loan of $600 from a two-month old baby to his parents when there were no witnesses.

JILLY COOPER (b. 1937; English writer and humorist)

From *Class*:

The most terrible story is told of the very shy wife who was bogged down at home by several little children, but who was invited to her husband's annual dinner-dance. As he was doing very well, she made a tremendous effort, buying a new dress, going to the hairdresser, arranging for her mother to baby-sit, and scouring the headlines for conversational fodder. The great day dawned and, on arriving at the dance, she discovered she was sitting next to her husband's boss. Despite her trepidation they got on terribly well and it was only during the main course, when suddenly everything went quiet, that she realized she had cut up all his meat for him.

PHYLLIS DILLER (b. 1919; American comedienne)

Cleaning your house while the kids are still growing
Is like shovelling the walk before it stops snowing.

NORA EPHRON (b. 1941; American writer)

From *Heartburn*:

If pregnancy were a book they would cut the last two chapters.

JEAN KERR (b. 1923; American playwright and essayist)

The real menace in dealing with a five-year-old is that in no time at all you begin to sound like a five-year-old.

DOROTHY PARKER (1893–1967; American writer, satirist and humorist)

From 'The Bolt behind the Blue':

'You don't know how I've always wanted to have a child all my own. Without having any old man mixed up in it.'

'I'm afraid that would be rather hard to accomplish,' Mrs Hazelton said. 'I guess you'd just have to take the bitter along with the sweet, like the rest of us . . .'

MARY ROBERTS RINEHART (1876–1958; American writer)

You're a perfect child, a stubborn child! Your mind's in pigtails, like your hair.

JOAN RIVERS (b. 1939; American comedienne)

A friend of mine confused her valium with her birth control pills – she had 14 kids but didn't give a shit.

FLORIDA SCOTT-MAXWELL (b. 1883; American writer and psychologist)

No matter how old a mother is she watches her middle-aged children for signs of improvement.

VICTORIA WOOD (b. 1953; English comedienne and writer)

From *Up to you, Porky*:

Let's face it, if God had meant men to have children, he would have given them pvc aprons.

CLOTHES

CHARLOTTE BINGHAM (b. 1942; English writer)

From *Coronet Among the Weeds*:

You only need one jumper if you're a beatnik. If you change your jumper you lose your identity.

ERMA BOMEBECK (b. 1927; American writer and humorist)

From *Motherhood: The Second Oldest Profession*:

A bridegroom's mother is supposed to wear beige and keep her mouth shut.

COLETTE (1873–1954; French novelist)

From *Gigi*:

Advice from a world-weary former courtesan to her schoolgirl niece: Don't ever wear artistic jewellery. It *wrecks* a woman's reputation.

MAVIS GALLANT (b. 1922; Canadian writer)

She has the loaded handbag of someone who camps out and seldom goes home . . .

MARGARET HALSEY (b. 1910; American writer)

Englishwomen's shoes look as if they had been made by someone who had often heard shoes described, but had never seen any.

JANICE JAMES (contemporary English journalist)

'The Bottom Line'

Though she wears expensive designer pants,
Her hips still look much bigger than her friend's,
And she only bought off-the-peg denims . . .
Sadly, though we may do our bumps and bends,
It's the genes,
Not the jeans,
That shape our ends!

DOROTHY PARKER (1893–1967; American writer, satirist and humorist)

Vogue fashion caption:

Brevity is the Soul of Lingerie.

BERYL PFIZER (20th c. American writer)

If the shoe fits, ask for it in another colour.

JOAN RIVERS (b. 1939; American comedienne)

Princess Di wears more clothes in one day than Gandhi wore in his entire life.

FREYA STARK (b. 1893; English travel writer)

There are few sorrows through which a new dress or hat will not send a little gleam of pleasure however fugitive.

SHELLEY WINTERS (b. 1922; American actress)

Nudity on stage? I think it's disgusting. But if I were 22 with a great body, it would be artistic, tasteful, patriotic and a progressive religious experience.

CONVERSATION

NANCY ASTOR (1879–1964; American-born British politician. First woman to take her seat in the House of Commons)

We women do talk too much, but even then we don't tell half we know.

APHRA BEHN (?1640–88; English novelist and playwright)
From *The Dutch Lover:*

I never made love so well as when I was drunk. It improves my parts and makes me witty; that is, it makes me say anything that comes next, which passes nowadays for wit.

MARGUERITE, COUNTESS OF BLESSINGTON (1789–1849; English writer and socialite)

Bores are people who talk of themselves when you are thinking only of yourself.

WENDY COPE (b. 1945; English poet)
From 'From June to December':

> It's nice to meet serious people
> And hear them explain their views:
> Your concern for the rights of women
> Is especially welcome news.
>
> I'm sure you'd never exploit one;
> I expect you'd rather be dead;
> I'm thoroughly convinced of it –
> Now can we go to bed?

MARY DUNN (1900–58; English writer and social satirist, best known for her 'Lady Addle' books)

Blanche, Lady Addle, remembers one of her mother's maxims (from *The World of Lady Addle*):

If the hostess is herself conscious of the same sensations [ennui or lack of conversation], she should say to her guests, 'If you will excuse me, I have to see the housekeeper about some jellies for the Almshouse.'

MARIA EDGEWORTH (1767–1849; English novelist)

The bore is usually considered a harmless creature, or of that class of irrational bipeds who hurt only themselves.

MARGARET HALSEY (b. 1910; American writer)

From *With Malice Towards Some*:

Listening to Britons dining out is like watching people play first-class tennis with imaginary balls.

LISA KIRK (b. 1925; American musical comedy artiste)

A gossip is one who talks to you about others; a bore is one who talks to you about himself; and a brilliant conversationalist is one who talks to you about yourself.

FRAN LEBOWITZ (b. 1951; American writer)

From *Metropolitan Life*:

Radio news is bearable. This is due to the fact that while the news is being broadcast the disc jockey is not allowed to talk.

LYDIA LOPOKOVA (1892–1981; Russian, Diaghilev ballet dancer and wife of economist John Maynard Keynes; often deliberately misused English to comic effect)

To Margot Asquith, at a luncheon party given by Lady St Just (Florrie Grenfell):

Margot dear, I had the most wonderful weekend recently at a country house where there were the most exotic birds, as well as the most beautiful *ovaries* I have ever seen.

LADY DOROTHY NEVILL (1826–1913; English writer and society hostess)

The real art of conversation is not only to say the right thing in the right places but to leave unsaid the wrong thing at the tempting moment.

DOROTHY PARKER (1893–1967; American writer, satirist and humorist)

At the reception of her remarriage to Alan Campbell:

People who haven't talked to each other in years are on speaking terms again today – including the bride and groom.

MAE WEST (1892–1980; American, 'world's greatest movie siren')

In reply to the 'chivalrous' statement, 'I never argue with a lady':

'Playing safe, huh?'

DEATH

DJUNA BARNES (1892–1982; American writer)

Describing preparing for a fake death scene (from 'The Jest of Jests'):

When a woman decides to lie down and play 'possum she always selects with fearful care her hosiery, her petticoats and her shoes.

CATHERINE BRAMWELL-BOOTH (b. 1883; English, grand-daughter of Salvation Army founder Bramwell-Booth)

One thing I shall miss in heaven is gardening. I don't know; we shan't have weeds in heaven, shall we?

BETTE DAVIS (b. 1908; American film actress)

When she was told that a rumour had started that she had died Miss Davis said firmly:

With the newspaper strike on I wouldn't even consider it.

TEXAS GUINAN (1878–1933; American nightclub hostess during Prohibition)

On herself (reportedly almost her last words):

I want to lie in state at Campbell's. I want for once to give the people a chance to see me without a cover charge.

MARY WILSON LITTLE (19th c.; American writer)

In some parts of Ireland the sleep which knows no waking is always followed by a wake which knows no sleeping.

BELLE LIVINGSTONE (1875–1957; American courtesan and actress, nicknamed The Belle of Bohemia)

The inscription she wished on her tombstone:

This is the only stone I have left unturned.

PRINCESS MARGARET (b. 1930)

Aged six, on the death of George V:

Grandpa has gone to heaven and I'm sure God is finding him very useful.

JESSICA MITFORD (b. 1917; English writer)

From *The American Way of Death*:

Alas, poor Yorick! How surprised he would be to see how his counterpart of today is whisked off to a funeral parlor and is in short order sprayed, sliced, pierced, pickled, trussed, trimmed, creamed, waxed, painted, rouged and neatly dressed – transformed from a common corpse into a Beautiful Memory Picture.

Quoting a radio commercial for an undertaker in *The American Way of Death*:

> If your loved ones have to go
> Call Columbus 690.
> If your loved ones pass away
> Have them pass the Chambers way.
> Chambers' customers all sing
> 'Death, oh death, where is thy sting?'

In an interview after the publication of *The American Way of Death*:

I have nothing against undertakers personally. It's just that I wouldn't want one to bury my sister.

DOROTHY PARKER (1893–1967; American writer, satirist and humorist)

Miss Parker and a group of friends were playing the old game of writing their own inscriptions for their future tombstones. Her suggestions for herself included: 'Excuse my dust'; 'This is on me'; and 'If you can read this, you've come too close.'

Describing an actress's tombstone (from 'Tombstones in the Starlight'):

> Her name, cut clear upon this marble cross,
> Shines as it shone when she was still on earth;
> While tenderly the mild, agreeable moss
> Obscures the figures of her date of birth.

On being informed of the death of the notoriously taciturn US President Calvin Coolidge:

How can they tell?

JEAN RHYS (1894–1979; English writer)
From *Good Morning, Midnight*:

Next week, or next month, or next year I'll kill myself. But I might as well last out my month's rent, which has been paid up, and my credit for breakfast in the morning.

THEADORA VAN RUNKLE (b. ?1949; American fashion designer)

Death is very sophisticated. It's like a Noel Coward comedy. You light a cigarette and wait for it in the library.

GLORIA SWANSON (1899–1983; American actress)
When I die, my epitaph should read: *She Paid the Bills*.

LILY TOMLIN (b. 1939; American actress)

There will be sex after death; we just won't be able to feel it.

MAUD BEERBHOM TREE (1863–1937; English comedy actress, wife of the actor Sir Herbert Beerbohm Tree)

When she lay dying in hospital, her lawyer came to see her to help her to put her affairs in order. After he had gone away, her daughter asked her if his visit had not too greatly tired her. 'Not at all,' said Lady Tree, 'He was just teaching me my death duties.'

DIVORCE

ILKA CHASE (1903–78; American writer and actress)

Ilka Chase had been married to Louis Calhern, who divorced her in order to marry Julia Hoyt. Sorting through her possessions shortly after the unhappy episode she found some visiting cards she had had printed for herself with the name Mrs Louis Calhern. Generously, and bearing in mind her own experience, she sent them on to the new Mrs Louis Calhern with a short note: 'Dear Julia, I hope these reach you in time.'

ZSA ZSA GABOR (b. ?1918; Hungarian-born actress; Miss Hungary 1936; seven times married)

I'm a wonderful housekeeper. Every time I get a divorce, I keep the house.

Zsa Zsa Gabor appeared as an 'agony aunt' on the early American television show 'Bachelor's Haven'. One deeply distressed viewer wrote to her saying, 'I am breaking off my engagement to a very wealthy man. He gave me a beautiful house, a mink coat, diamonds, a stove and an expensive car. What shall I do?'

'Send back the stove,' advised Miss Gabor.

SORAYA KHASHOGGI (b. 1941; Leicestershire-born ex-wife of Saudi Arabian billionaire Adnan Khashoggi)

On being told that her (now ex-) husband Robert Rupley was seen living it up in London with a blonde:

Never mind about my husband, where's my Lamborghini?

MARY WILSON LITTLE (19th c.; American writer)

It is difficult to tell which gives some couples the most happiness, the minister who marries them or the judge who divorces them.

CLARE BOOTHE LUCE (b. 1903; American writer, politician and diplomat)

From *The Women*:

Child: The only good thing about divorce – you get to sleep with your mother.

DOROTHY PARKER (1893–1967; American writer, satirist and humorist)

On her husband, the day of her decree absolute:

Oh, don't worry about Alan . . . Alan will always land on somebody's feet.

In 'Dusk Before Fireworks' a couple are discussing a call from the husband's mistress:

He dropped wearily into the low chair. 'She says she has something she wants to tell me.'

'It can't be her age,' she said.

He smiled without joy. 'She says it's too hard to say over the wire,' he said.

'Then it may be her age,' she said. 'She's afraid it might sound like her telephone number.'

HELEN ROWLAND (1875–1950; American writer)

From *Reflections of a Bachelor Girl*:

Love, the quest; Marriage, the conquest; Divorce, the inquest.

BARBARA STANWYCK (b. 1907; American actress)

I'm supposed to be a hermit, a loner nursing a broken heart because I lost Robert Taylor . . . My divorce from Taylor was sixteen years ago. If I'd been holding a torch that long by now my arm would have withered.

CAROLYN WELLS (1869–1942; American writer and humorist)

The wages of sin is alimony.

EXERCISE

PAM AYRES (contemporary English writer of humorous verse)

From 'How I Loved You, Ethel Preedy, with Your Neck so Long and Slender':

> How I loved you, Ethel Preedy,
> With your neck so long and slender.
> At the Tennis Dance
> What magic charm did you engender!
> Our eyes met in the crowd,
> Your fingers tightened on the racquet,
> But when I tore my gaze away
> Some swine pinched me jacket.

ERMA BOMBECK (b. 1927; American writer and humorist)

From *Motherhood: The Second Oldest Profession*:

She dropped out of aerobics class when the only thing she could touch were her knees to her chest . . . and only because her chest met her knees halfway.

PHYLLIS DILLER (b. 1917; American comedienne)

Excusing herself from taking exercise:

I'm at an age when my back goes out more than I do.

RACHEL HEYHOE FLINT (b. 1937; former England women's cricket captain)

On how to get the 2,000 women's cricket clubs together with the 20,000 men's cricket clubs:

All we need is an extra lavatory and a broom cupboard.

GRETA GARBO (b. 1905; legendary Swedish film actress)
Asked by gossip columnist Louella Parsons if her relaxation really was to swim in the nude:

What's wrong with that? Have you ever known of a fish to wear a swimsuit?

VIRGINIA GRAHAM (b. 1912; American writer)

Good shot, bad luck and hell are the five basic words to be used in tennis.

MAUREEN LIPMAN (b. 1946; English actress and writer)
From *How Was It for You?*:

At present my idea of a good work-out is a two-hour worry about the bags under my eyes, but in the past I have dabbled in leg warmerland with the best of them. In fact many's the morning you might have glimpsed me on the way out of my Lotte Berk muscle-tightening class, blithely attempting to walk unaided to my car, both legs shaking so violently that I am forced to seek support from passing wing mirrors.

LIZ LOCHHEAD (b. 1947; Scottish poet and revue writer)
'Scotch Mist (The Scotsport Song)'

Lazy Sunday Afternoon in Central Scotland.
You scoosh 'Yes please'
Behind your knees
And ask him what he's got planned?
All over Central Scotland, men are pulling down the blinds.
The men of Central Scotland got something
Sort of Sunday Afternoonish on their minds.

Match of the day, action replay it's on Scotsport.
Chuck us a can, a man's not a man without Scotsport.

You can cook good, you can look good
You can play hard to get.
To turn him on's impossible –
He's turning on the set.
He'll never tell you he loves you
Unless he's pissed.
Love in a Cold Climate,
Scotch Mist!

Pissed off with life
Your average wife
Is quite entitled to feel
He's a waste of a bottle of Bad-E-Das
And a damned good meal.
He'll say, after Scotsport
You're next on the list.
Love in a Cold Climate,
Scotch Mist!

RUTH MCKENNEY (1911–72; American writer)

From *Guinea Pig*:

Eileen and I were very bored rowing around in the dark, and finally, in desperation, we began to stand up and rock the boat, which resulted, at last, in my falling into the lake with a mighty splash.

When I came up, choking and mad as anything, Eileen saw me struggling, and, as she always says with a catch in her voice, she only meant to help me. Good intentions, however, are of little importance in a situation like that. For she grabbed an oar out of the lock, and with an uncertain gesture hit me square on the chin.

I went down with a howl of pain. Eileen, who could not see much in the darkness, was now really frightened. The cold water revived me after the blow and I came to the surface, considerably weakened but still able to swim over to the boat. Whereupon Eileen, in a noble attempt to give me the oar to grab, raised it once again, and socked me square on the top of the head. I went down again, this time without a murmur, and my last thought was a vague wonder that my own sister should want to murder me with a rowboat oar.

As for Eileen, she heard the dull impact of the oar on my head and saw the shadowy figure of her sister disappear. So she jumped in the lake, screeching furiously, and began to flail around in the water, howling for help and looking for me. At this point I came to the surface and swam over to the boat, with the intention of killing Eileen.

JOAN RIVERS (b. 1939; American comedienne)

I'm Jewish. I don't work out. If God wanted us to bend over he'd put diamonds on the floor.

PAM SHRIVER (b. 1962; American tennis player)

The only way to beat Martina [Navratilova] now, is to run over her foot in the car park.

MAE WEST (1892–1980; American, 'world's greatest movie siren')

On Marilyn Monroe's marriage to Joe DiMaggio:

Why marry a ballplayer when you can have the whole team?

FAME

JULIE ANDREWS (b. 1935; English actress and singer)

During the making of *Torn Curtain*, Alfred Hitchcock complained that a spotlight was 'making a hell of a line over her head'. Miss Andrews, who used to specialise in playing fresh English rose stereotypes, retorted, 'That's my halo'.

SARAH BERNHARDT (1844–1923; French tragedienne)

When she toured the United States Bernhardt's performances and choice of 'unsuitable' plays caused clergymen of all persuasions to denounce her, with the result that she received much invaluable publicity. To one particular vociferous opponent, the Bishop of Chicago, she sent the following note: 'Your excellency, I am accustomed when I bring an attraction to town, to spend $400 on advertising. As you have done half the advertising for me, I herewith enclose $200 for your parish.'

INA CLAIRE (1895–1985; American actress)

Ina Claire was a well-known stage actress who successfully made a break into the early 'talkies' of Hollywood. For a brief three years she was married to John Gilbert, idol of the silent movies. One day a movie magazine reporter asked her how it felt to be married to a celebrity.

'You'd better ask my husband,' was Miss Claire's reply.

TEXAS GUINAN (1878–1933; American nightclub hostess during Prohibition)

She once lamented that when she was a dancer, before she found fame as a club hostess, she was 'So far back in the chorus they had to take a brick out of the wall to find me.'

HELEN HAYES (b. 1900; American actress and writer)

In 1955, on the news that a theatre was to be renamed after her:

An actress's life is so transitory – suddenly you're a building.

CLARE BOOTHE LUCE (b. 1903; American writer, politician and diplomat)

On the writing of memoirs:

All autobiographies are alibi-ographies.

AGNES DE MILLE (b. 1908; American choreographer, dancer and writer, daughter of film magnate Cecil B. de Mille)

Theatre people are always pining and agonizing because they're afraid that they'll be forgotten. And in America they're quite right. They will be.

JANE RUSSELL (b. 1921; American film actress)

Sometimes the photographers would pose me in a low-necked

nightgown and tell me to bend down and pick up the pails. They were not shooting the pails.

NORMA TALMADGE (1897–1957; American star of silent screen)

Approached by a fan a few years after her retirement in 1930:

'Get away, dear,' she bellowed, 'I don't need you anymore.'

ELIZABETH TAYLOR (b. 1932; English film actress)

On rumours she would be posing for *Playboy*:

Oh sure – and next month I'm dressing up as a sea bass for the front cover of *Field and Stream*!

RAQUEL WELCH (b. 1940; American actress)

I feel people are trying to bury me in a sea of C-cups.

FAMILIES

QUEEN ELIZABETH THE QUEEN MOTHER (b. 1900; wife of King George VI)

The queen was taking her daughter, the young Princess Margaret Rose, for a walk when they were approached by an over-familiar but well-meaning lady. Rushing up to them the lady gushed, 'So this is the dear little lady we've all heard so much about!' Recoiling slightly Princess Margaret began to remonstrate, 'I'm *not* a little lady, I'm a princ . . .' At which point the Queen interrupted her, saying, 'She's not *quite* a little lady yet. But she's learning.'

ZSA ZSA GABOR (b. ?1918; Hungarian-born actress; Miss Hungary 1936; seven times married)

I believe in large families. Every woman should have at least three husbands.

BEATRICE LILLIE (LADY PEEL) (b. 1898; Canadian-born comedy actress)

From *Every Other Inch A Lady*:

I'll simply say here that I was born Beatrice Gladys Lillie at an extremely tender age because my mother needed a fourth at meals.

ALICE ROOSEVELT LONGWORTH (1884–1980; American, daughter of President Theodore Roosevelt; nicknamed 'Princess Malice')

On her father, from whom she inherited her exhibitionist tendencies: Father wanted to be the corpse at every funeral, the bride at every wedding, and the baby at every christening.

LYDIA LOPOKOVA (1892–1981; Russian, Diaghilev ballet dancer and wife of economist John Maynard Keynes; often deliberately misused English to comic effect)

Proposing the health of her hostess, Florrie Grenfell, at a party: And let us not forget dear Florrie's mother, who compiled her.

MRS H. MEADE

Out of the mouths of babes come things you wouldn't want your neighbours to hear.

ETHEL WATTS MUMFORD (1878–1940; American writer and humorist)

God gives us our relatives; thank God we can choose our friends!

BERYL PFIZER (20thc American writer)

On 'junk' TV:

No matter what the critics say, it's hard to believe that a television program which keeps four children quiet for an hour can be all bad.

JOAN RIVERS (b. 1939; American comedienne)

I said to my mother-in-law, 'My house is your house.' She said, 'Get the hell off my property.'

QUEEN VICTORIA (1819–1901)

I fear the seventh grand-daughter and fourteenth grandchild becomes a very uninteresting thing – for it seems to me to go on like the rabbits in Windsor Park.

KATHARINE WHITEHORN (contemporary English writer and broadcaster)

From 'Mother' [a parody of Rudyard Kipling's 'Tommy']

I went into the kitchen to get a cup o' tea
The boys they stopped their talking and their eyes all said to me
'Look, can't you see we've friends in?' and they 'eaved a pointed sigh.
I climbed the staircase back to bed and to myself sez I:

    Oh, it's Mummy this and Mummy that and 'Mummy, do you *mind*!'
    But it's 'Mummy, can you help me?' when your boots are hard to find,
    'I've left my football kit at home, so could you bring it round?
    'Oh thanks, that's grand – and by the way – you haven't got a pound?'

We're Mums, so we're the cleaners too, the washers and the cooks;
An' they think that's all we're good for, once we've lost our dolly looks.
My 'usband doesn't mind to say I'm just a silly moo,
But 'e sees it all quite different when 'e wants my wages too.

    Oh it's 'Mum's too slow' and 'Mum's too fat' and 'Mum's a bleeding fool,'
    But it's 'Mum could make some money' once the kids are off to school.
    They want us scrubbing saucepans and they think that's all we do –
    But they call us 'Superwoman' when they want our wages too.

FOOD

TALLULAH BANKHEAD (1902–68; American actress, also known for her outrageous lifestyle)

I never eat on an empty stomach.

ISABELLA BEETON (1836–65; English journalist and cookery writer)

From *Mrs Beeton's Book of Household Management*:

It is generally established as a rule not to ask for soup or fish twice, as, in so doing, part of the company may be kept waiting too long for the second course, when, perhaps, a little revenge is taken by looking at the awkward consumer of the second portion.

MADELEINE BINGHAM (b. 1912; English writer)

I've always thought Alfred showed a marked lack of ingenuity over cakes – why didn't he cut off the burned bits, and ice the rest?

ERMA BOMBECK (b. 1927; American writer and humorist)

From *Motherhood: The Second Oldest Profession*:

I got so much food spit back in my face when my kids were small, I put windshield wipers on my glasses.

MRS PATRICK CAMPBELL (1865–1940; English actress)

At supper Mrs Pat (Stella) asks for a 'Belle Elmore' (from *Mrs Pat* by Margot Peters):

The footman paled. Belle Elmore had been the wife of the notorious Dr Crippen, who had quite recently murdered, dismembered, and buried her in small pieces under his pantry floor . . . Hoping he had not heard correctly the footman dared to repeat the question. 'But I've told you once, my good man,' said Stella, breaking off conversation with her neighbour and looking up, annoyed. 'I said a Belle Elmore. Surely you know what a Belle Elmore is! A mixed grill of course. Marrow bones, tongue, some liver, brains, kidneys.'

TEXAS GUINAN (1878–1933; American nightclub hostess
during Prohibition)

On fighting a constant battle with her weight problem, at one
stage losing 5 stones:

I go up and down the scale so often that if they ever perform an
autopsy on me they'll find me like a strip of bacon – a streak of
lean and a streak of fat.

FLORENCE KING (b. 1936; American writer and critic)

From *Confessions of a Failed Southern Lady*:

[My mother's] idea of breakfast was coffee and cigarettes, so
Herb cooked his own bacon and eggs. Her other specialities,
culled in bridal haste from Depression-era newspapers, were
mock chicken salad, which involved a can of tuna fish; and mock
salmon loaf, which involved a can of tuna fish and a bottle of
pink vegetable coloring. When Herb, oblique as always,
suggested a mockless Friday, she fixed him a hot dog.

FRAN LEBOWITZ (b. 1951; American writer)

From *Social Studies*:

A great many people in Los Angeles are on strict diets that
restrict their intake of synthetic foods. The reason for this
appears to be a widely-held belief that organically grown fruit
and vegetables make the cocaine work faster.

BELLE LIVINGSTONE (1875–1957; American courtesan and
actress, nicknamed The Belle of Bohemia)

From *Great Dining Disasters*:

At a feast given by the Egyptian millionaire Ibrahim Bey Cherif
(at which she was the only woman) Belle Livingstone watched a
hundred naked dervishes wheel themselves into self-hypnosis
and then bite the heads off live snakes, plunge red-hot swords
through their cheeks and eat cactus stalks. For 'desert', they
crunched through thick glass tumblers. Asked if there was
anything more she could suggest for the meal, she replied: 'A

glass of brandy . . . And I hope Allah appreciates all this.'

MARIE LLOYD (1870–1922; English cockney music hall star)
From *Our Marie* by Naomi Jacobs:

Marie Lloyd was entertaining some fellow artistes at a large hotel outside Glasgow. The soup was really terrible and Marie insisted on seeing the manager.

'Unless you're keeping it a dead secret – what is this?' she asked.

'Soup, madam.'

Marie said: 'There you are – you said it was, didn't you, Clare? Now, tell me, what kind of soup is it?'

'Pea soup, madam.'

'Pea soup? Now I'm something of a cook and I'm going to give you a hint. When you want to make pea soup, be reckless; use *three* peas and damn the expense.'

EMILY LOTNEY
Quoted in *Quotations For Our Time*:

A converted cannibal is one who, on Friday, eats only fishermen.

SHIRLEY LOWE AND ANGELA INCE (contemporary English writers)
Describing a 'nouvelle cuisine' dinner party (from *Losing Control*):

Arranged on our plates were some tiny little crustaceans (shrimp probably, but it was so small it might just as well have been baby scorpion) encased in pale pink aspic. Flanking it on one side were four shavings of carrot, on the other, intricately carved wedges of celery. These little fragments lay in a pool of that thin, watery tomato sauce, so fashionable just then, which gave the impression that the hostess, overwrought by anxiety and the labour of giving a dinner party, had slashed her wrists while dishing up.

DOROTHY PARKER (1893–1967; American writer, satirist and humorist)

Asked if she had enjoyed a party:

Enjoyed it? One more drink and I would be under the host.

RUTH S. SCHENLEY (American writer)

Little snax
Bigger slax.

ALICE B. TOKLAS (1877–1968; American writer, companion of Gertrude Stein)

From *The Alice B. Toklas Cook Book*:

What is sauce for the goose may be sauce for the gander, but is not necessarily sauce for the chicken, the duck, the turkey or the guinea hen.

MAE WEST (1892–1980; American, 'world's greatest movie siren')

I did make coffee once, after sendin' out for instructions. But then I got otherwise involved in somethin' more interestin' and forgot to turn off the heat. Well – I never turn off the heat.

VICTORIA WOOD (b. 1953; English comedienne and writer)

I always thought *Coq au Vin* was love in a lorry.

From *Up to you, Porky*:

She's a nice girl, but when someone chain-smokes Capstan Full Strength and wears a coalman's jerkin, you're hardly tempted to sample their dumplings.

GOSSIP

MARGOT ASQUITH (1864–1945; English socialite and political hostess, wife of Prime Minister Herbert Asquith)

Of a friend:

She tells enough white lies to ice a cake.

MYRTIE LILLIAN BARKER (b. 1910; American writer and journalist)

The idea of strictly minding our own business is moldy rubbish. Who could be so selfish?

MARIA EDGEWORTH (1767–1849; English novelist)

I hate scandal – at least I am not so fond of it as the lady of whom it was said she could not see the poker and tongs standing together without suspecting something wrong!

GEORGE ELIOT (1819–80; English novelist)
From *The Mill on the Floss*:

The happiest woman, like the happiest nations, have no history.

AMANDA LEAR (b. ?1944; English model and singer)

I hate to spread rumours – but what else can one do with them?

LIZ LOCHHEAD (b. 1947; Scottish poet and revue writer)
From 'True Confessions' (*Rap*):

> Our conversations range from the Arts to Child Psychology
> From World Affairs and Who Cares
> To Avant-Garde Gynaecology.
> I know her trouble with her nerves
> and the trouble with her mate;
> What she did with her brother when they were eight;
> and Should-she-love him? Should-she-leave him?
> What-were-their-Chances?;
> the night she was almost tempted by lesbian advances
> I know about the strange stains she found
> on young Sebastian's pyjamas;
> her Wild Night with that waiter
> on her trip to the Bahamas;
> I get the dope on each High Hope;
> on her fainting spasms;

the ins-and-outs of her orgasms.
How the Pill gives her Headaches;
her cramps with the coil;
how My-Man-once-made-this-pass-at-her-at-a-party-but
She Was Too Loyal.

ALICE ROOSEVELT LONGWORTH (1884–1980; American,
daughter of President Theodore Roosevelt; nicknamed 'Princess
Malice')

If you haven't got anything good to say about anyone come and
sit by me.

ELIZABETH MONTAGU (1720–1800; English writer and
prominent 'Blue Stocking')

In a letter to the Duchess of Portsmouth:

The Dowager Duchess of Norfolk bathes, and being very tall she
had like to have drowned a few women in the Cross Bath, for she
ordered it to be filled till it reached to her chin, and so all those
who were below her in stature, as well as rank, were forced to
come out or drown.

DOROTHY PARKER (1893–1967; American writer, satirist and
humorist)

Praising a mutual friend:

You know she speaks eighteen languages, and she can't say *no* in
any of them.

From *Tombstones in the Starlight*:

> IV. The Fisherwoman
> The man she had was kind and clean
>   And well enough for every day
> But, oh, dear friends, you should have seen
>   The one that got away!

DIANE DE POITIERS (Duchesse de Valentinois) (1499–1566;
French writer, mistress of Henry II of France)

The years that a woman subtracts from her age are not lost. They are added to other women's.

AGNES REPPLIER (1855–1950; American essayist)

Conversation between Adam and Eve must have been difficult at times because they had nobody to talk about.

ELLA WHEELER WILCOX (1850–1919; American writer)

> Have you heard of the terrible family They,
> and the dreadful venomous things They say?
> Why, all the gossip under the sun
> If you trace it back you will find begun
> In that wretched house of They.

LADY (ANNE) WILSON (19th c.; Scottish-born writer who lived for 20 years in India)

From *Letters From India*:

Speculating that the rosy cheeks and bronze-tinted hair of an acquaintance might not be entirely due to nature:

Perish the thought but let me first give it expression!

GUILT

NANCY ASTOR (1879–1964; American-born British politician. First woman to take her seat in the House of Commons)

In passing, also, I would like to say that the first time Adam had a chance he laid the blame on woman . . .

ANN B. CAESAR (American writer)

A tip is a small sum of money you give to someone because you are afraid he wouldn't like not being paid for something you haven't asked him to do.

AGNES GUILFOYLE

On confession:

Good for the soul – but bad for the heel.

FRAN LEBOWITZ (b. 1951; American writer)

In New York it's not whether you win or lose – it's how you lay the blame.

BELLE LIVINGSTONE (1875–1957; American courtesan and actress, nicknamed The Belle of Bohemia)

On attending her first formal dinner before the First World War (from *Belle of Bohemia*):

At table my mother was on one side of me and a young man on the other; hardly were we seated than I felt my mother's foot steal across near mine to be in readiness to press down on it should the occasion arise, as though it might have been the pedal of a piano. Further disapproval she was bound to signal by pinching my arm. When I drained off the yellow water at my plate I felt a pedal thrust and a pinch, but later, as I almost fainted on finding a piece of mouldy cheese on my plate, which the butler had served me while I was talking, she nearly pressed my foot down through the Turkish rug, and catching her eye, I knew I had to swallow the smelly lump of awfulness spread over a water cracker; clutching for another glass of the sparkling liquid, I drained it, despite her frantic pedalling and pinching.

This, my first dinner party, commenced my hatred of formal gatherings, but since then I have cultivated a taste for both champagne and Roquefort cheese . . .

ELAINE MAY (contemporary American comedienne and film writer)

In an improvised sketch as an adulterous wife:

I feel so guilty – he's my husband – he trusts me. If he didn't trust me I couldn't do this.

DOROTHY PARKER (1893–1967; American writer, satirist and humorist)

After having an abortion:

It serves me right for putting all my eggs in one bastard.

In 1963 (when she was 70):

If I had any decency, I'd be dead. Most of my friends are.

JOAN RIVERS (b. 1939; American comedienne)

I saw my first porno film recently – a Jewish porno film – one minute of sex and nine minutes of guilt.

CAROLYN WELLS (1869–1942; American humorist and writer)

A guilty conscience is the mother of invention.

KATHARINE WHITEHORN (contemporary English writer and broadcaster)

I just wish, when neither of us has written to my husband's mother, I didn't feel so much worse about it than he does.

HAPPINESS

INGRID BERGMAN (1915–82; Swedish film actress)

Happiness is good health and a bad memory.

PAULETTE GODDARD (b. 1911; American film actress)

If all the stock markets of the world were to collapse, diamonds would still survive. So what's all the panic about?

XAVIERA HOLLANDER (b. ?1936; Dutch prostitute, 'The Happy Hooker')

There is only one other profession that outranks bankers as dedicated clients, and that is the stockbroker . . . When the stocks go up, the cocks go up!

LYDIA LOPOKOVA (1892–1981; Russian, Diaghilev ballet dancer and wife of economist John Maynard Keynes)

On taking long walks over the Sussex Downs:

When I am on the Downs in the morning I feel that I am having a cocktail with God.

AMY LOWELL (1874–1925; American poet and critic)

Happiness, to some elation;
Is to others, mere stagnation.

PHYLLIS MCGINLEY (1905–78; American writer and essayist)

A bookworm in bed with a new novel and a good reading lamp is as much prepared for pleasure as a pretty girl at a college dance.

SOPHIE TUCKER (1884–1966; Jewish-American vaudeville and nightclub entertainer)

On her staying power at the age of sixty:

I'm as tough as ever. What's the secret? Doing what the doctor tells you. I've cut out smoking and drinking. All I have left is gin rummy – they can't take that away from me.

HOLLYWOOD

JULIE ANDREWS (b. 1935; English actress and singer)

On Joyce Haber, a Los Angeles columnist who liked to make snide comments about her:

They should give Haber open-heart surgery – and go in through the feet.

NANCY BANKS-SMITH (contemporary English television critic)

It is axiomatic in American mini-series that no child ever has the slightest idea who his father or mother is and therefore stands in constant peril of marrying his grandmother. The most striking instance of this was Bare Essence in which the hero, Chase, turned out to be the son of his grandfather and, therefore, his own uncle. His mother, discovering that she was her son's sister-in-law, died of confusion.

VICKI BAUM (1888–1960; American writer)

What I like about Hollywood is that one can get along by

knowing two words of English – swell and lousy.

CONSTANCE BENNETT (1904–65; American actress)
On Marilyn Monroe:
There is a broad with a future behind her.

CANDICE BERGEN (b. 1946; American actress and
photographer)
Hollywood is like Picasso's bathroom.

FANNY BRICE (1891–1951; American comedienne and Ziegfeld
Follies star)
On Esther Williams, aquatic star of films such as *Million Dollar
Mermaid* and *Dangerous When Wet*:
Wet she's a star – dry she ain't.

DOROTHY GISH (1898–1968; American silent film actress)
Turning down a Paramount offer of one million dollars to make
eight comedy films:
Oh no, to have a million dollars at my age might ruin my
character.

TEXAS GUINAN (1878–1933; American nightclub hostess
during Prohibition)
Hollywood sounds like something for a Christmas decoration –
but it's just Western for poison ivy.

Commenting on the mental attributes of the Hollywood
directors she had worked with:
They go around carrying a chip on their shoulders – which is a
true indication of wood a little higher up.

IRENE HANDL (b. 1901; English actress and novelist)
Oh yes, I've been to Hollywood . . . I was there for, ooh, twenty-
four hours.

KATHARINE HEPBURN (b. 1909; American film actress)
Told by Otto Preminger on a radio chat show:

Katharine Hepburn was dining with Otto Preminger when producer Joseph Schenck came in and said, 'Miss Hepburn, how come in all these years in Hollywood, we never met?'

'Mr Schenck, I consider that one of the great achievements of my life,' was Miss Hepburn's immediate response.

ANITA LOOS (1888–1981; American novelist and screen writer)

A leader of public thought in Hollywood wouldn't have sufficient mental acumen anywhere else to hold down a place in the bread line.

If Hollywood ever wants to film a supercolossal epic of its own, it couldn't do better than to settle for the private life of Joseph M. Schenck.

ELAINE MAY (contemporary American comedienne and film writer)

In an improvised sketch mocking the Hollywood craze for 'cast of thousands' epics:

My latest film is MGM's latest and greatest biblical spectacular . . . This will be the biblical spectacular to end all biblical spectaculars . . . It is called THE BIG SKY and it's The Life Story of God!

BETTE MIDLER (b. 1945; American actress, comedienne and singer)

From *A View from A Broad*:

If you live in Beverly Hills they don't put blinkers in your car. They figure if you're that rich you don't have to tell people where you're going.

LOUELLA PARSONS (1881–1972; American Hollywood columnist)

When she heard that Errol Flynn's present to his new fiancée was a package of French snails, laced with garlic sauce, she remarked, 'She is the first girl I've ever seen to lead Errol Flynn by the nose.'

BARBARA STANWYCK (b. 1907; American actress)

After her husband Robert Taylor had been boasting about the

number of hours he had chalked up flying:

Now you can do everything the birds can do except sit on a barbed wire fence.

HUSBANDS

SIMONE DE BEAUVOIR (1908–86; French author)

To catch a husband is an art, to keep him a job.

FANNY BRICE (1891–1951; American comedienne and Ziegfeld Follies star)

On her jailed husband, Nick Arnstein, who was said to have masterminded a half-million dollar robbery:

Masterminded! He couldn't mastermind an electric light bulb into the socket.

JANE WELSH CARLYLE (1801–66; English letter-writer, wife of historian Thomas Carlyle)

The Carlyles were miserably married but Jane Carlyle refused to admit defeat. When her husband was more than somewhat enamoured of Lady Ashburton she wrote: 'People who are so dreadfully devoted to their wives are so apt, from mere habit, to get devoted to other people's wives as well.'

CHER (b. 1945; American singer and actress)

The trouble with some women is they get all excited about nothing – and then marry him.

DAME AGATHA CHRISTIE (1891–1975; English crime fiction writer)

An archaeologist is the best friend any woman can have; the older she gets, the more interested he is in her.

LADY (JENNIE) CHURCHILL (1851–1921; American, mother of Sir Winston Churchill)

On her marriage to Montagu Porch in 1918 (he was forty-one, three years younger than her son Winston):

He has a future and I have a past, so we should be all right.

ZSA ZSA GABOR (b. ?1918; Hungarian-born actress; Miss Hungary 1936; seven times married)

Husbands are like fires. They go out when unattended.

TEXAS GUINAN (1878–1933; American nightclub hostess during Prohibition)

Miss Guinan made extravagant claims about the number of times she had been married and the outstanding characteristics of her husbands. Of her first (and, in fact, only) husband she gave the following opinion: 'If my poor, dear, departed husband were alive, he would have made a grand aviator – he was no good on earth!'

MURIEL HUMPHREY (b. 1912; American, wife of Hubert Humphrey, US Democratic Senator)

When her husband had made an overlong speech:

Hubert, to be eternal, you don't have to be endless.

ERICA JONG (b. 1942; American writer)

Bigamy is having one husband too many. Monogamy is the same.

CAROLE LOMBARD (1908–42; American film actress who married Clark Gable)

As promised she sent a cable to her friends on her honeymoon with husband no. 2, William Powell. It read: 'Nothing new to report.'

ANITA LOOS (1888–1981; American novelist and screen writer)
From *Gentlemen Prefer Blondes*:

. . . I have not wasted all of my time on Henry, even if I do not marry him, because I have some letters from Henry which would come in very, very handy if I did not marry Henry. So Dorothy seems to agree with me quite a lot, because Dorothy says the only thing she could stand being to Henry, would be to be his widow at the age of 18.

JOAN RIVERS (b. 1939; American comedienne)

I asked my husband to restore my confidence. My boobs have gone, my stomach's gone, say something nice about my legs. He said, 'Blue goes with everything.'

HELEN ROWLAND (1875–1950; American writer)

From *The Rubaiyat of a Bachelor*:

A husband is what is left of the lover after the nerve has been extracted.

ADELA ROGERS ST JOHNS (b. 1894; American journalist and writer)

I think every woman's entitled to a middle husband she can forget.

MARGARET THATCHER (b. 1925; English politician, first female UK Prime Minister)

Arriving at a domestic airport during her election campaign Mrs Thatcher and her husband, Denis, somehow became separated.

'Where's Denis?' asked one of her aides.

'I expect he's trying to get some duty frees,' was the tart reply.

MAUD BEERBOHM TREE (1863–1937; English comedy actress, wife of the actor Sir Herbert Beerbohm Tree)

From *Distinguished Company* by John Gielgud:

Her husband emulated a number of his contemporaries in siring offspring besides those already presented him by his wife. Lady Tree, playing hostess, was once heard to remark, 'Ah, Herbert, late again? Another confinement in Putney?'

INNUENDO

SOPHIE ARNOULD (1740–1802; French opera singer)

To an actress who was bemoaning the fact that she was so near to her fortieth birthday:

Courage, my dear, console yourself with the thought that every day takes you further away from it.

The 'admirer' of a young actress had given her a diamond necklace in the style sometimes known as a *rivière* (river). Being overlong it had a tendency to disappear into the recipient's cleavage, prompting Mme Arnould to remark tartly, 'The river is merely trying to return to its source.'

MARGOT ASQUITH (1864–1945; English socialite and political hostess, wife of Prime Minister Herbert Asquith)

'Margott,' said blonde film siren Jean Harlow when they were first introduced, 'how lovely to meet you.'

   'My dear,' replied Lady Asquith, 'the "t" is silent – as in Harlow.'

TALLULAH BANKHEAD (1902–68; American actress, renowned for her husky Southern drawl)

One day the writer Earl Wilson, whose voice happened to be of a considerably higher pitch than Tallulah's, telephoned her for an interview. One of his questions was, 'Are you ever mistaken for a man on the phone?'

   To which Tallulah retorted, 'No, darling, are you?'

ERMA BOMBECK (b. 1927; American writer and humorist)

Any college that would take your son he should be too proud to go to.

DAME LILIAN BRAITHWAITE (1873–1948; English actress noted for her comedy roles)

At a magnificent party to celebrate a long run she pointed to her dress with the remark, 'C. [the producer] has given me a dear little diamond brooch . . . can you see it?'

CAROLINE OF ANSPACH (1683–1737; wife of King George II)

Queen Caroline was very popular but died prematurely. As the

King sobbed by her bedside she advised him to marry again.

George, overcome by emotion, demurred, 'Never. I shall have mistresses instead.'

'That shouldn't make any difference,' was her cynical reply.

LILLIAN CARTER (1898–1983; mother of 39th US President Jimmy Carter)

On Johnny Carson:

I thought he was an ass until I met him.

MARION DAVIES (1898–1961; American mistress of William Randolph Hearst)

Hearst come, Hearst served.

RACHEL HEYHOE FLINT (b. 1937; former England women's cricket captain)

Commenting on a packet of frozen pastry she had bought bearing the legend, 'Makes a pie for four people, or 12 little tarts':

I hadn't realised that it would be such a good opportunity to invite the current England women's cricket team.

NELL GWYNN (1650–87; English actress and mistress of Charles II)

To her great chagrin, Nell Gwynn, unlike her rival, the Duchess of Portsmouth, had failed to extract a title from Charles II in return for services rendered. One day Nell arrived at Court in an extremely expensive gown which provoked the Duchess's snide remark, 'Why, woman, you are fine enough to be a queen.'

'You are entirely right, madam,' retorted Nell, 'and I am whore enough to be a duchess!'

LILLIAN HELLMAN (1905–84; American playwright and writer)

On Norma Shearer:

A face unclouded by thought.

FANNY HOLMES (1841–1929; wife of US Supreme Court Judge Oliver Wendell Holmes, Jnr)

When President Roosevelt asked the newly arrived judge's wife whether she found the other Washington wives interesting, she replied cautiously: 'Washington is full of famous men and the women they married when young.'

LYDIA LOPOKOVA (1892–1981; Russian, Diaghilev ballet dancer and wife of economist John Maynard Keynes; often deliberately misused English to comic effect)

Before meeting the granddaughter of Charles Darwin, the man who wrote about the theory of evolution, she was 'primed' with an explanation of his book, *The Origin of Species*, but when the moment came she simply exclaimed: 'So you are the granddaughter of the man who wrote Genesis!'

Lydia attended the baptism of a baby whose mother had been seen 'in the company of' Osbert Sitwell. Peering hard into the crib, she remarked: 'It doesn't *look* like Osbert!'

MOMS MABLEY (20th c. American comedienne)

A woman is a woman until the day she dies, but a man's a man only as long as he can.

EDNA ST VINCENT MILLAY (1892–1950; American poet)

While she was staying with Somerset Maugham at his Mediterranean villa, Noel Coward, Beverly Nichols and Godfrey Winn were invited for lunch. When she was introduced to them, on the terrace overlooking the sea where they were to eat, she exclaimed: 'Oh, Mr Maugham, but this is fairyland!'

DOROTHY PARKER (1893–1967; American writer, satirist and humorist)

On hearing that a well-known English actress, famous for her love affairs with members of the legal profession, had broken her leg, she surmised: 'She must have done it sliding down a barrister.'

When she heard two lesbians discussing whether or not they needed or should be allowed the benefits of a marriage ceremony, Dorothy Parker was quick to offer some salient advice: 'Of course you must have legal marriages. The children have to be considered.'

JOAN RIVERS (b. 1939; American comedienne)

About Teddy Kennedy, whose political career was permanently blighted by the Chappaquiddick incident:

When he lost the Democratic nomination to Jimmy Carter he said, 'Let bygones be bygones.' Then he offered to drive him home!

Joan Collins – I said she was known on the show as the British Open.

JACQUELINE SUSANN (1918–74; American popular novelist)

Jacqueline Susann wrote very successful 'sexy' novels. When her best-seller *The Love Machine* was on the point of being overtaken by Philip Roth's novel *Portnoy's Complaint*, a book in which masturbation is a major feature, she was asked for her opinion of its author. Her answer was: 'He's a fine writer, but I wouldn't want to shake hands with him.'

MAE WEST (1892–1980; American, 'world's greatest movie siren')

I have my moments [pause] . . . they're all weak ones.

DAME REBECCA WEST (1892–1983; English novelist and critic)

On a New York socialite and his young man friend who went everywhere dressed in identical outfits:

They look like a nest of tables.

INSULTS

MARGOT ASQUITH (1864–1945; English socialite and political hostess, wife of Prime Minister Herbert Asquith)

About a friend:

She's as tough as an ox. She'll be turned into Bovril when she dies.

From *Distinguished Company* by John Gielgud:

My favourite story (told me by Frederick Ashton) is of Margot standing defiantly in the hall at the reception given for some smart society wedding, muttering to the guests as they arrived: 'Don't go upstairs. The bride's hideous.'

TALLULAH BANKHEAD (1902–68; American actress, also known for her outrageous lifestyle)

Alexander Woollcott, a leader of the Algonquin 'Round Table' (which prided itself on its sophistication and witty conversation) had invited Tallulah to attend one of their luncheons. After taking it all in for a few moments she turned to him and said: 'Mr Woollcott, there is less here than meets the eye.'

ETHEL BARRYMORE (1879–1959; American actress)

A woman invited to dinner with Ethel Barrymore failed to turn up on the appropriate evening and compounded her rudeness by failing to write or telephone with an apology or explanation. Unfortunately for her she came face to face with Ethel at an art gallery a week or so later. Awkwardly she launched into her excuses.

'I believe I was supposed to join you for dinner last Tuesday,' she began.

'Oh, really?' cut in Ethel promptly. 'And did you come?'

SARAH BERNHARDT (1844–1923; French tragedienne)

Bernhardt and Oscar Wilde violently disagreed over the interpretation of her role during rehearsals for one of his plays. Hoping to calm things down Oscar asked, 'Would you mind if I smoke?'

'I don't care if you burn,' was the encouraging reply.

DAME LILIAN BRAITHWAITE (1873–1948; English actress noted for her comedy roles)

James Agate, the drama critic, introduced himself to Lilian

Braithwaite at a party saying somewhat tactlessly, 'For a long time I have wanted to tell you I regard you as the second-best actress in London.'

'I'm so flattered to hear that,' she replied crushingly, 'from the second-best drama critic in London.'

COMTESSE DE BREMONT (fl. 1890s; French writer)

The Comtesse de Brémont asked for an interview with W.S. Gilbert, and was told that she would have to pay twenty guineas for the privilege. Thereupon she wrote to him in these terms: 'The Comtesse de Brémont presents her compliments to Mr W.S. Gilbert and in reply to his answer to her request for an interview for St Paul's in which he states his terms as twenty guineas for that privilege, begs to say that she anticipates the pleasure of writing his obituary for nothing.'

MRS PATRICK CAMPBELL (1865–1940; English actress)

After listening to Henry Arthur Jones in his cockney accent read his interminable latest play, *Michael and His Lost Angel*:

But it's so *long*, Mr Jones, even *without* the *h*'s!

From *Mrs Pat* by Margot Peters:

Stella [Mrs Campbell] went to visit the actor Allan Pollock in the hospital. He had been frightfully injured – his face shot away; and now surgeons were grafting what amounted to a new one. Stella demanded that he remove the bandages and let her see his ravaged face. Pollock refused.

'I've lost a son in this war and I have the right to look,' she insisted.

Pollock shook his head; the sight, he told her, would be too horrible.

'Nonsense, man,' retorted Stella, tears channelling her face powder, 'I have just left Lady Tree.'

LADY VIOLET BONHAM CARTER (1887–1969; English Liberal politician)

On Sir Stafford Cripps:

Sir Stafford has a brilliant mind, until it is made up.

JOYCE GRENFELL (1910–79; English comedienne and writer)

Friends of mine inherited a large, heavy, Victorian house and gradually, room by room, they redecorated the place. At last the dining room was done exactly as they wanted it and to celebrate the completion of the work they gave a dinner party. As the assembled company moved into the new room, one of the guests stopped in the doorway and said: 'Heavens! What fun you'll have doing up *this* room.'

GRACE HIBBARD (?1870–1911; American poet and writer)

> 'An Honest Lawyer' – book just out –
>   What can the author have to say?
> Reprint perhaps of ancient tome –
>   A work of fiction anyway.

ROSAMOND LEHMANN (b. 1905; English writer)

About Ian Fleming (quoted in Mark Amory (ed.), *The Letters of Ann Fleming*):

[He] got off with women because he could not get on with them.

ALICE ROOSEVELT LONGWORTH (1884–1980; American, daughter of President Theodore Roosevelt; nicknamed 'Princess Malice')

On President Harding, recently deceased:

He was not a bad man. He was simply a slob.

On Calvin Coolidge:

He looks as if he had been weaned on a pickle.

ANITA LOOS (1888–1981; American novelist and screen writer)

When black-haired Louise Brooks, famous for her strange, almost bi-sexual appearance, was miscast as the gold-digging blonde Lorelei Lee in the film version of *Gentlemen Prefer Blondes*, Lorelei's creator Anita Loos swiftly had her thrown off the picture with the crushing remark: 'If I ever write a part for a cigar-store Indian, you'll get it.'

LADY MARY WORTLEY MONTAGU (1689–1762; English letter-writer, notable for her *Letters from the East*, written while her husband was Ambassador at Constantinople in 1716; pioneer of smallpox vaccine)

To Alexander Pope who specialised in satirical poetry:

Satire should, like a polished razor keen,
Wound with a touch that's scarcely felt or seen.
Thine is an oyster knife, that hacks and hews;
The rage but not the talent to abuse.

LA WANDA PAGE (contemporary American comedienne)

On the occasion of a dinner to honour George Burns:

George, you're too old to get married again. Not only can't you cut the mustard, honey, you're too old to open the jar.

DOROTHY PARKER (1893–1967; American writer, satirist and humorist)

Although newspaper magnate William Randolph Hearst and his mistress, the actress Marion Davies, lived together as man and wife, he made it a rule that no unmarried couples should sleep together at their San Simeon hideout. When Dorothy Parker was spending the weekend there she broke the rule and was summarily despatched from the house. On her way out she signed the visitors' book with the following rhyme:

> Upon my honor
> I saw a Madonna
> standing in a niche
> Above the door
> Of the famous whore
> Of a prominent son of a bitch.

JOAN RIVERS (b. 1939; American comedienne)

On Bo Derek:

She turned down the role of Helen Keller – she couldn't remember the lines . . . She's so stupid she returns bowling balls because they've got holes in them.

Boy George is all England needs – another Queen who can't dress.

Marie Osmond – she's so pure Moses couldn't part her knees.

DAME EDITH SITWELL (1887–1966; eccentric English poet)

Virginia Woolf's writing is no more than glamorous knitting. I believe she must have a pattern-book.

CORNELIA OTIS SKINNER (1901–79; American actress and writer)

When Cornelia Otis Skinner was playing the lead in George Bernard Shaw's play *Candida*, he sent her a telegram – 'Excellent. Greatest.' Immediately she cabled back – 'Undeserving such praise.' Back came Shaw's response – 'I meant the play.' To which she sent her reply – 'So did I.'

MAE WEST (1892–1980; American, 'world's greatest movie siren')

Come up and see me sometime. Come up Wednesday. That's amateur night.

After meeting Bette Davis:

Two years ago I met Garbo. Now I've met you. I'm so thrilled, I'm goin' home, rest up a couple of days and then concentrate on meetin' the new quarterback at USC.

After meeting Miss Davis a second time, she remarked to her escort: 'Well, dear, I think we've had the best of her.'

W.C. Fields, the cynical American comedian, had persuaded Mae West to make a film with him. She agreed on condition that Fields, a notorious drunk, did not touch alcohol on the set. Unfortunately he found he could not cope with life without drink and was soon appearing for work drunk despite his good intentions. Miss West, who took pride in not mincing her words, ordered his removal with the memorable line: 'Pour him out of here.'

PEGGY WOOD (b. 1892; American actress)

Alexander Woollcott was discussing a possible revival of *Macbeth* on Broadway when Peggy came unexpectedly into the room.

'We're discussing the cast,' he told her, 'but I don't think you'd make a very good Lady Macbeth, do you, Peggy?'

'No, Alec,' she agreed, 'but you would.'

JOKES

JEANINE BURNIER (contemporary American comedienne)

I worked for a while as a stripper – that's when I realised I had a flair for comedy.

MRS PATRICK CAMPBELL (1865–1940; English actress)

On being told by a member of her adoring public that her performance had been a 'tour de force':

I suppose that is why I am always forced to tour.

PAULINE DANIELS (b. 1955; English comic on the Northern Clubs circuit)

'Quick, quick,' I told him as he came into the kitchen 'I want you to make mad passionate love to me.'

'Why now?' he said.

'Because I want to cook an egg and I don't like them to boil for more than 27 seconds!'

GEORGE ELIOT (1819–80; English novelist)

From *Daniel Deronda*:

A difference of taste in jokes is a great strain on the affections.

ELLIE LANE (b. 1964; English comedienne)

This guy comes home from work and starts packing.

'What are you doing?' his wife asked him.

'I'm going to Fiji – I've heard the women there pay you £5 every time they make love to you.'

'Right, I'm coming with you.'

'Whatever for?'

'I want to see how you're going to live on £10 a month.'

BETTE MIDLER (b. 1945; American actress, comedienne and singer)

I will never forget it! It was on the occasion of Ernie's eightieth birthday. He rang me up and said, 'Soph! Soph! I just married me a twenty-year-old girl. What do you think of that?' I said to him, 'Ernie, when I am eighty I shall marry me a twenty-year-old boy. And let me tell you something, Ernie: twenty goes into eighty a helluva lot more than eighty goes into twenty!'

MAUREEN LIPMAN (b. 1946; English actress and writer)

At the Woman of the Year Lunch, 28 October 1985:

'What does a Jewish princess make for dinner? Reservations!'

GERTRUDE STEIN (1874–1946; American/French writer)

From *Everybody's Autobiography*:

I understand you undertake to overthrow my undertaking.

DAME SYBIL THORNDIKE (1882–1976; English actress)

A story recounted by the British broadcaster Richard Baker:

Not long before she died I went to interview Dame Sybil for BBC Radio's 'Start the Week'. When I arrived at the block of flats in Chelsea where she lived, the hall porter said, 'Good morning Mr Baker. I'm sorry to tell you Dame Sybil has had a fall.'

'Oh, then I won't bother her now,' I said.

'Oh, but you must go up,' said the porter. 'Dame Sybil's companion wants you to help get her up.'

I went up to the flat and was told Dame Sybil had fallen out of bed. We went into the bedroom where the great lady was indeed on the floor beside her bed, but ebulliently cheerful as always.

'Oh, I'm so glad you've come,' she said. 'What a pickle I'm in! You didn't know I was a fallen woman, did you?'

MAE WEST (1892–1980; American, 'world's greatest movie siren')

On the RAF naming their life jackets after her:

Sorta makes me feel like I started muh own second front. I've been in *Who's Who*, 'n' I know what's what, but it's the first time I ever made a dictionary.

On one of her Christmas cards:

Santa Comes But Once a Year – too Bad!

Outside Grauman's Chinese Theater for the premiere of *I'm No Angel*:

It's nice to be in a place where they take your footprints rather than your fingerprints.

To a suitor reciting her physical attributes:

Wait a minute! Wait a minute! Is this a proposal or are you taking an inventory?

KATHARINE WHITEHORN (contemporary English writer and broadcaster)

Outside every thin girl there's a fat man trying to get in.

PAULA YATES (b. 1960; English television presenter)

Her tongue-in-cheek introduction to Bob Geldof and the Boomtown Rats – he has been her live-in lover for over five years:

I'm not allowed to introduce the next band, in case people think I'm giving the lead singer one.

KINDNESS

DAME LILIAN BRAITHWAITE (1873–1948; English actress noted for her comedy roles)

Of French actress Yvonne Arnaud as she entered middle age:

It's still the dear little face we all loved so in *Candle Light* [pause] – but there's another face round it.

DOROTHY DIX (1909–70; pioneer English woman lawyer)

Drying a widow's tears is one of the most dangerous occupations known to man.

MRS GASKELL (1810–65; English novelist)

From *Cranford*:

[We] talked on about household forms and ceremonies, as if we all believed that our hostess had a regular servants' hall . . . instead of the one little Charity School maiden, whose short ruddy arms could never have been strong enough to carry the tray up-stairs, if she had not been assisted in private by her mistress, who now sat in state, pretending not to know what cakes were sent up, though she knew, and we knew, and she knew that we knew, and we knew that she knew we knew, she had been busy all the morning making tea-bread and sponge cakes.

BARONESS BETTINA VON HUTTEN (1874–1957; American/English writer)

A good many women are good-tempered simply because it saves the wrinkles coming too soon.

VIVIAN YEISER LARAMORE (b. 1891; American poet)

Talk to me tenderly, tell me lies;
I am a woman and time flies.

ALICE ROOSEVELT LONGWORTH (1884–1980; American, daughter of President Theodore Roosevelt; nicknamed 'Princess Malice')

On herself at 80:

I'm just an amiable, kindly old thing, as I've always been. I was born a kindly, old thing. If anyone takes that seriously, Hah! My speciality is detached malevolence.

DOROTHY PARKER (1893–1967; American writer, satirist and humorist)

From 'The Wonderful Old Gentleman':

But Mrs Whittaker's attitude of kindly tolerance was not confined to her less fortunate relatives. It extended to friends of her youth, working people, the arts, politics, the United States in general, and God, Who had always supplied her with the best of service. She could have given Him an excellent reference at any time.

JOAN RIVERS (b. 1939; American comedienne)

On Motown singing star Stevie Wonder:

Who's going to tell him that he's got a macramé plant holder on his head?

MAE WEST (1892–1980; American, 'world's greatest movie siren')

Look after these men – give them all my address.

LIFE

POLLY ADLER (1900–62; highly successful American 'madam', on whom the play *The Greatest Little Whorehouse in Texas* was based)

I am one of those people who just can't help getting a kick out of life – even when it's a kick in the teeth.

LOUISA MAY ALCOTT (1832–88; American writer, author of *Little Women*)

Now I am beginning to live a little, and feel less like a sick oyster at low tide.

MINNA ANTRIM (b. 1861; American writer, fl. early 20th c.)

Experience is a good teacher, but she sends in terrific bills.

PAM AYRES (contemporary English writer of humorous verse)

From 'Oh no, I got a Cold':

> I burnt me bit of dinner

'Cause I've lost me sense of smell,
But then, I couldn't taste it,
So that worked out very well.
I'd buy some, down the café
But I know that at the till
A voice from work will softly say,
'I thought that you were ill.'

TALLULAH BANKHEAD (1902–68; American actress, also
known for her outrageous lifestyle)
From *Tallulah*:

Here's a rule I recommend. Never practise two vices at once.

It's the good girls who keep diaries; the bad girls never have the
time.

LILIAN BAYLIS (1874–1937; English music-hall singer and
founder of the Old Vic)
Life – with a capital F.

SHIRLEY CONRAN (b. 1932; English writer)
Life is too short to stuff a mushroom.

MME A.M. BIGOT DE CORNUEL (1605–94; French socialite)
No man is a hero to his valet.

MARIA EDGEWORTH (1767–1849; English novelist)
All work and no play makes Jack a dull boy,
All play and no work makes Jack a mere toy.

GEORGE ELIOT (1819–80; English novelist)
Nothing is as good as it seems beforehand.

ELINOR GLYN (1864–1943; English novelist and Hollywood
scriptwriter famous for her erotic writing)
Life is short – avoid causing yawns.

RUTH GORDON (1896–1984; American actress)

I think there is one smashing rule – never face the facts.

JERRY HALL (b. ?1956; American model)

There are three secrets my mother told me. Be a maid in the living room, a cook in the kitchen – and a whore in the bedroom. I figure as long as I have a maid and a cook I'll do the rest myself. You can only do so much in one day.

LILLIAN HELLMAN (1905–84; American playwright and writer)

God forgives those who invent what they need.

CHRISTINE KEELER (b. 1942; English, former call-girl at the centre of the 1963 Profumo scandal)

Discretion is the polite word for hypocrisy.

JEAN KERR (b. 1923; American playwright and essayist)

The average, healthy, well-adjusted adult gets up at 7.30 in the morning feeling just plain terrible.

ISOBEL LENNART (1915–71; American playwright and film writer)

From *Funny Girl* (based on the life of Jewish-American comedienne Fanny Brice):

Fanny: Look – suppose all you ever had for breakfast was onion rolls. All of a sudden one morning, in walks a bagel. You'd say, 'Ugh! What's that?' Until you tried it. *That's* my trouble. I'm a bagel on a plate full of onion rolls!

MARIE LLOYD (1870–1922; English cockney music-hall star)

You could cover a sow's ear with silk purses, and the damn bristles would still work through.

MYRNA LOY (b. 1902; American film actress)

They say the movies should be more like life. I think life should be more like the movies.

EDNA ST VINCENT MILLAY (1892–1950; American poet)

> It is not true that life is one damn thing after another – it's one damn thing over and over.

> My candle burns at both ends;
> It will not last the night;
> But ah, my foes, and oh, my friends –
> It gives a lovely light!

MARGARET MITCHELL (1900–49; American writer)

From *Gone With the Wind*:

Death and taxes and childbirth! There's never any convenient time for any of them!

ETHEL WATTS MUMFORD (1878–1940; American writer and humorist)

On reading Robert Burns's 'To a Louse':

> [O wad some Pow'r the giftie gie us
> To see oursels as others see us!]:
> Oh wad some power the giftie gie us
> To see some people before they see us.

FLORENCE NIGHTINGALE (1820–1910; English, Crimean War nurse)

In 1864, after the Crimean War was over, she wrote:

My life now is as unlike my hospital life as reading a cookery book is unlike a good dinner.

DOROTHY PARKER (1893–1967; American writer, satirist and humorist)

> 'One Perfect Rose'

> Why is it no one ever sent me yet
> One perfect limousine, do you suppose?
> Ah no, it's always just my luck to get
> One perfect rose.

> Life is a glorious cycle of song,

A medley of extemporania;
And love is a thing that can never go wrong,
And I am Marie of Rumania.

IRENE PETER
Quoted in *Quotations For Our Time*:
Ignorance is no excuse – it's the real thing.

ROSALIND RUSSELL (b. 1911; American film actress)
Flops are a part of life's menu and I've never been a girl to miss out on any of the courses.

MRS A. SIMMONS (American, 20th c.)
Quoted in *Bartlett's Unfamiliar Quotations*:
The early bird wishes he'd let someone else get up first!

ELIZABETH W. SPALDING
People differ. Some object to the fan dancer, and others to the fan.

LILY TOMLIN (b. 1939; American actress)
We're all in this together – by ourselves.

MAE WEST (1892–1980; American, 'world's greatest movie siren')
It's better to be looked over than overlooked.

VICTORIA WOOD (b. 1953; English comedienne and writer)
A man is designed to walk three miles in the rain to phone for help when the car breaks down – and a woman is designed to say, 'You took your time' when he comes back dripping wet.

LITERATURE

MRS PATRICK CAMPBELL (1865–1940; English actress)
On Noel Coward:
His characters talk like typewriting.

DAME AGATHA CHRISTIE (1891–1975; English crime fiction writer)

I've always believed in writing without a collaborator, because where two people are writing the same book, each believes he gets all the worries and only half the royalties.

JILLY COOPER (b. 1937; English writer and humorist)
From *Class*:

My favourite mini-cab driver has a theory that tall people are good in bed because only they can reach the sex books that librarians insist on putting on the top shelves.

ANABEL COWAN (contemporary American writer)
Quoted in *Bartlett's Unfamiliar Quotations*:

While Christmas shopping, I asked a pretty college freshman in our local bookstore during the holiday rush for a copy of Dickens' *Christmas Carol*. Smiling sweetly she said, 'Oh, he didn't write songs – he wrote books.'

HELENE HANFF (contemporary American writer)
A story told by Valerie Grove in the *Spectator*, 17 August 1985:

When she was last in London she was as usual on a literary pilgrimage – visiting Dickens's house, Keats's house, etc. As we happened to be near Hampstead and she had just been seeing 'Tinker Tailor Soldier Spy' on television, I asked would she like to see John le Carré's house? She certainly would. So I drove into his crescent and stopped at his gate, whereupon to my horror the writer himself emerged on his doorstep, wrapping a scarf about his neck. He stared hard at us and we stared back.

'That was *him*!' I said to Miss Hanff.

'Wahl,' she drawled, impressed. 'That was something. They showed me Keats's house – but they never showed me Keats!'

FLORENCE KING (b. 1936; American writer and critic)
From *Confessions of a Failed Southern Lady*:

There's something unrefined about a reading woman, they always reek of the lamp.

ANITA LOOS (1888–1981; American novelist and screen writer)
From *Gentlemen Prefer Blondes*:

I did intend to luncheon at the Ritz with Dorothy today and of course Coocoo had to spoil it, as I told him that I could not luncheon with him today, because my brother was in town on business and had the mumps, so I really could not leave him alone. Because of course if I went to the Ritz now I would bump into Coocoo. But I sometimes almost have to smile at my own imagination, because of course I have not got any brother and I have not even thought of the mumps for years. I mean it is no wonder that I can write.

JOANNA LUMLEY (b. 1946; English model and actress)
After she had been one of the judges for the prestigious British literary award, the Booker Prize:

To be a judge you don't have to know about books, you have to be skilled at picking shrapnel out of your head.

NANCY MITFORD (1904–73; English novelist and biographer)
From *The Pursuit of Love*:

I have only read one book in my life, and that is *White Fang*. It's so frightfully good I've never bothered to read another.

DOROTHY PARKER (1893–1967; American writer, satirist and humorist)

And I'll stay off Verlaine too; he was always chasing Rimbauds.

As artists [lady novelists] they're rot, but as providers they're oil wells – they gush.

Miss Parker reviewed books for the *New Yorker* under the pseudonym 'Constant Reader'. When asked to review A.A. Milne's whimsical children's classic *The House at Pooh Corner* she summarised her views in the short phrase: 'Tonstant weader fwowed up.'

AMANDA MCKITTERICK ROS (1860–1939; English novelist and poet in the style of William McGonagall)

On publishers:

They love to keep the Sabbath – and everything else they can lay their hands on.

DAME EDITH SITWELL (1887–1966; eccentric English poet)

A great many people now reading and writing would be better employed in keeping rabbits.

FRANCES TROLLOPE (1780–1863; English writer and mother of the novelist Anthony Trollope; her best-known book is *Domestic Manners of the Americans*)

When taxed with the fact that most of her characters were unflattering portraits of her own acquaintances she replied: 'I always pulp my acquaintances before serving them up. You would never recognise a pig in a sausage.'

VIRGINIA WOOLF (1882–1941; English novelist)

I would venture to guess that Anon, who wrote so many poems without signing them, was often a woman.

LOVE

ELLEN DOROTHY ABB (American writer, fl. 1937)
From *What Fools We Women Be*:

It may be love that makes the world go round, but it's spinsters who oil the wheels.

MARGUERITE, COUNTESS OF BLESSINGTON (1789–1849; English writer and socialite)

Love matches are made by people who are content, for a month of honey, to condemn themselves to a life of vinegar.

COLETTE (1873–1954; French novelist)

A liaison of seven years is like following a husband to the colonies; when you come back no one recognizes you and you've forgotten how to wear your clothes properly.

From *Break of Day*:

My true friends have always given me that supreme proof of
devotion, a spontaneous aversion for the man I loved.

MARLENE DIETRICH (b. 1902; German singer and actress)

Grumbling is the death of love.

PHYLLIS DILLER (b. 1917; American comedienne)

The romance is dead if he drinks champagne from your slipper
and chokes on a Dr Scholl's foot pad.

CAROL ANN DUFFY (b. 1955; English playwright and poet)

From 'The Businessman's Love Poem':

Last Autumn, and the first Beaujolais Nouveau
    était arrivé. I parked the new Metro
near the wine bar where I had a rendezvous.
    Inside, I saw you.

I remember old man Perkins doing a spiel
    on Sinclairs; the dainty way you ate your veal.
Your perfect lips, slowly sipping at your drink,
    were F.T. pink.

It knocked me for six, that smile like Perrier
    poured over ice. And then, in profile, the way
you looked like Chrissie Lloyd! I toyed with my quiche.
    Were you out of reach?

A face like yours could sell a million floppy
    discs, change hardened admen into optimists.
You were as beautiful as low inflation,
    as tax evasion.

I wondered what your name was. Rosemary?
    What lucky chap you worked for? Or maybe
you were Schedule D, an independent MS
    I wanted to ks.

I knew you'd like opera, theatre, the ballet,
    was certain you'd bathe with Roger et Gallet.

I hoped you'd like Henley, Glyndebourne and sports cars
    and my Eau Sauvage.

Then at the wordprocessor, I sat alone
    and typed. The face which stared at me, my own,
crumpled like an old pound note with fading life.
    went home to its wife.

A face like yours could sell a million floppy
    discs, change hardened admen into optimists.
You were as beautiful as low inflation,
    as tax evasion.

BARONESS MARIE VON EBNER-ESCHENBACH (1830–1916)

We don't believe in rheumatism and true love until after the first attack.

ZSA ZSA GABOR (b. ?1918; Hungarian-born actress; Miss Hungary 1936; seven times married)

I always say a girl must get married for love – and just keep on getting married until she finds it.

TEXAS GUINAN (1878–1933; American nightclub hostess during Prohibition)

Marriage is alright, but I think it's carrying love a little bit too far.

JOYCE MCKINNEY (b. 1950; American)

In court, charged with kidnapping a twenty-one-year-old Mormon missionary, her former lover, Kirk Anderson:

For the love of Kirk, I would have skied down Everest in the nude with a carnation up my nose.

DOROTHY PARKER (1893–1967; American writer, satirist and humorist)

If nobody had ever learned to undress, very few people would be in love.

SARAH SIDDONS (1755–1831; English tragedienne)

Sarah Siddons was one of the Kembles, a prominent English theatrical family. Possibly because he knew the problems so well, her father, rather surprisingly, forbade her ever to marry an actor. When Sarah fell in love with William Siddons, a very minor member of her father's troupe, he was furious.

'How could you?' he demanded. 'Not only is he a member of our profession but quite the least talented in the company.'

'Precisely,' replied Sarah. 'You certainly couldn't call him an actor.'

THRYA SAMTER WINSLOW (1903–61; American writer and critic)

Platonic love is love from the neck up.

MARRIAGE

ZOË AKINS (1886–1958; American writer)

From *Daddy's Gone A-Hunting*:

Shutting one's eyes is an art, my dear. I suppose there's no use trying to make you see that – but that's the only way one *can* stay married.

NANCY ASTOR (1879–1964; American-born British politician. First woman to take her seat in the House of Commons)

When someone commented on the advantages she gained by marrying a rich man:

I married beneath me – all women do.

JANE AUSTEN (1775–1817; English novelist)

From *Emma*:

A woman is not to marry a man merely because she is asked or because he is attached to her, and can write a tolerable letter.

From *Mansfield Park*:

I think it ought not to be set down as certain, that a man must be acceptable to every woman he may happen to like himself.

From *Mansfield Park*:

There certainly are not so many men of large fortune in the world, as there are pretty women to deserve them.

From *Sense and Sensibility*:

'Oh! dear! one never thinks of married men being beaux – they have something else to do.'

From *Sense and Sensibility*:

His temper might perhaps be a little soured by finding, like many others of his sex, that through some unaccountable bias in favour of beauty, he was the husband of a very silly woman – but she [Elinor] knew that this kind of blunder was too common for any sensible man to be lastingly hurt by it.

From *Pride and Prejudice*:

It is a truth universally acknowledged, that a single man in possession of a good fortune, must be in want of a wife.

AMELIA BARR (1831–1919; English writer who lived in America)
From *Jan Vedder's Wife*:

'Is she not handsome, virtuous, rich, amiable?' they asked. 'What hath she done to thee?' The Roman husband pointed to his sandal. 'Is it not new, is it not handsome and well made? But none of you can tell where it pinches me.' That old Roman and I are brothers. Everyone praises 'my good wife, my rich wife, my handsome wife,' but for all that, the matrimonial shoe pinches me.

STEPHANIE BEACHAM (b. ?1949) English actress)
People keep asking me if I'll marry again. It's as if when you've had one car crash you want another.

ERMA BOMBECK (b. 1927; American writer and humorist)
From *Motherhood: The Second Oldest Profession*:

Married. It was like a dream come true for Donna. Just think, soon her little girl would have unpaid bills, unplanned babies, calls from the bank and sub-standard housing. All the things a mother dreams of for her child.

'BILL' CAGNEY (wife of American actor James Cagney)
After celebrating their Diamond Wedding in 1982:

You know, we've stayed married for so long that I think I'm going to charge folks a dollar a time to come and look at us.

MRS PATRICK CAMPBELL (1865–1940; English actress)
The deep, deep peace of the double bed after the hurly-burly of the chaise-longue.

MARIE CORELLI (1855–1924; English popular novelist)
Quoted in *Picking on Men*:

I never married because there was no need. I have three pets at home that answer the same purpose as a husband. I have a dog that growls every morning, a parrot that swears all afternoon and a cat that comes home late at night.

BETTE DAVIS (b. 1908; American film actress)
Would I consider remarriage? If I found a man who had $15,000,000, would sign over half of it to me before marriage, and guarantee he'd be dead within a year.

QUEEN ELIZABETH II (b. 1926)
At the Guildhall lunch celebrating her 25th wedding anniversary in 1972:

I am sure that on this day you will concede that I should begin with the words, 'My husband and I . . .'

ANN FLEMING (b. 1913; wife of the novelist Ian Fleming)
In a letter to Ian Fleming in 1962:

. . . if you were well and we were both younger our marriage would be over.

ZSA ZSA GABOR (b. ?1918; Hungarian-born actress; Miss Hungary 1936; seven times married)

A man in love is incomplete until he has married. Then he's finished.

I haven't known any open marriages, though quite a few have been ajar.

JUDY GARLAND (1922–69; American singer and actress)

To Artie Shaw, after his marriage to Lana Turner:

Artie, she's a nice girl, but it's like sitting in a room with a beautiful vase.

CHARLOTTE PERKINS STETSON GILMAN (1860–1935; American feminist writer)

> 'Queer People'
>
> The people people work with best
>   Are often very queer,
> The people people own by birth
>   Quite shock your first idea;
> The people people choose for friends
>   Your common sense appall,
> But the people people marry
>   Are the queerest ones of all.

ELLEN GLASGOW (1874–1945; American writer)

From *The Voice of the People*:

What a man marries for's hard to tell, an' what a woman marries for's past findin' out.

TEXAS GUINAN (1878–1933; American nightclub hostess during Prohibition)

I've been married once on the level, and twice in America.

VIRGINIA CARY HUDSON (1894–1954; American 'prodigy' who wrote her collection of essays *O Ye Jigs & Juleps!* aged ten)

I guess walking slow getting married is because it gives you time to maybe change your mind.

JEAN KERR (b. 1923; American playwright and essayist)

Marrying a man is like buying something you've been admiring for a long time in a shop window. You may love it when you get it home, but it doesn't always go with everything in the house.

FLORENCE KING (b. 1936; American writer and critic)
From *Confessions of a Failed Southern Lady*:

The only thing about marriage that appealed to me was sex without scandal: husbands could be counted on not to ask, 'How come you let me go all the way?'

CAROLE LOMBARD (1908–42; American film actress)
On her marriage to William Powell:

That son of a bitch is acting even when he takes his pajamas off.

SOPHIA LOREN (b. 1934; Italian film actress)
After receiving the certificate of her official marriage to Carlo Ponti, in France, April 1966:

It's a little like reading a theatre programme long after you've seen the show.

CLARE BOOTHE LUCE (b. 1903; American writer, politician and diplomat)
On the marriage of a particularly fertile couple:

It's what you might call an *enceinte cordiale*.

JAYNE MANSFIELD (1932–67; American film actress)

I got married and we had a baby nine months and ten seconds later.

LADY MARY WORTLEY MONTAGU (1689–1762; English letter-writer, best known for her *Letters from the East*, written while her husband was Ambassador at Constantinople in 1716; pioneer of smallpox vaccine)

Be plain in dress, and sober in your diet;
In short, my Dearie – kiss me, and be quiet.

DOROTHY PARKER (1893–1967; American writer, satirist and humorist)

Miss Parker was a regular contributor to the *New Yorker*. Even while she was on honeymoon the editor was pursuing her for her copy but on this occasion he received the following cryptic note: 'Too fucking busy, and vice versa.'

MOLLY PARKIN (b. 1932; English actress and writer)
From 'Familiarity':

We'll travel the world, hand in hand we'll go far.
We can stay at your brother's and borrow his car.

I'll give you my all, everything I will share.
Spent next week's housekeeping! Just you take care.

Dressed in those clothes you remind me of Spring.
The film will have started, wear any old thing.

We'll have a boy with a brain, a girl as sweet as sugar.
Good heavens, woman, what's gone wrong with your figure!

I live for your moods, sweet tears without cause.
What the hell are you on? The damned menopause?

HELEN ROWLAND (1875–1950; American writer)

Before marriage a man declares that he would lay down his life to serve you; after marriage, he won't even lay down his newspaper to talk to you.

From *Reflections of a Bachelor Girl*:

When you see what some girls marry, you realize how they must hate to work for a living.

From *Personally Speaking*:

Marriage is the only thing that affords a woman the pleasure of company and the perfect sensation of solitude at the same time.

LADY TROUBRIDGE (fl. early 1900s–46; English writer)
From *The Millionaire*:
A girl can't analyze marriage – and a woman daren't.

MAE WEST (1892–1980; American, 'world's greatest movie siren')
On marriage:
Only as a last resort.

He [William Randolph Hearst] wanted romance . . . I could have married him, but I was busy.

Marriage is a great institution, but I'm not ready for an institution yet.

KATHARINE WHITEHORN (contemporary English writer and broadcaster)
. . . a good marriage is like Dr Who's Tardis, small and banal from the outside, but spacious and interesting from within.

MRS WOODROW WILSON (born Edith Bolting Galt; 1872–1961; 2nd wife of US President Woodrow Wilson)
When Woodrow proposed to me I was so surprised I nearly fell out of bed.

MEDICINE

DR ELIZABETH GARRETT ANDERSON (1836–1917; first woman to practise medicine in England)
Elizabeth Garrett Anderson only treated women and children, and in reply to a gentleman who wanted to ask her 'if gout were in her line', she wrote: 'Dear Sir, gout is very much in my line, gentlemen are not.'

ERMA BOMBECK (b. 1927; American writer and humorist)

Never go to a doctor whose office plants have died.

PHYLLIS DILLER (b. 1917; American comedienne)

Health – what my friends are always drinking to before they fall down.

QUEEN ELIZABETH THE QUEEN MOTHER (b. 1900; wife of King George VI)

On a medical statement saying she was 'comfortable' following an operation in 1966:

There is all the difference in the patient's meaning of the word and the surgeon's.

HELENE HANFF (contemporary American writer)

From *Q's Legacy*:

After hearing she had to have a cataract operation:

Fact One: Cataract surgery is simple, painless and (except with implants) risk free . . . the whole procedure is common, routine and nothing to worry about.

Fact Two: Fact One applies only to cataracts on the eyes in somebody else's head.

JEAN KERR (b. 1923; American playwright and essayist)

One of the most difficult things to contend with in a hospital is the assumption on the part of the staff that because you have lost your gall bladder you have also lost your mind.

MAUREEN LIPMAN (b. 1946; English actress and writer)

From *How Was It For You?*:

During a memorable period, when we were both visiting a dental hospital for gum treatment, the nightly flossing, single-head and double-head brushing, plaque disclosing and mouth washing took so long it became a whole new form of contraception.

ALICE ROOSEVELT LONGWORTH (1884–1980; American, daughter of President Theodore Roosevelt; nicknamed 'Princess Malice')

After having her second breast removed at the age of eighty-six she quipped: 'I'm the only topless octogenarian in Georgetown.'

DOROTHY PARKER (1893–1968; American writer, satirist and humorist)

While recovering from an operation Dorothy Parker called her secretary in to the hospital to help her catch up on her correspondence. To the secretary's surprise, before they set to work, she pressed the button marked 'Nurse' and then explained: 'This way no one will come near us for at least forty-five minutes.'

JOAN RIVERS (b. 1939; American comedienne)

When I was in labour the nurses would look at me and say, 'Do you still think blondes have more fun?'

DAME EDITH SITWELL (1887–1966; eccentric English poet)
From *The Two Doctors*:

> When Doctor Dougall attended a funeral,
> The horse would gallop, as if in eagerness,
> As if his master had at last,
> Been granted his reward.

JILL TWEEDIE (b. 1936; English columnist and writer)

On a visit to the dentist (from *More From Martha: Further Letters from a Faint-hearted Feminist*)

Trouble with you, I said to him, is you're into S and I'm not into M.

MAE WEST (1892–1980; American, 'world's greatest movie siren')

On the fact that doctors would object to her two high colonics per day:

Sure, why wouldn't they? If you never get sick, how are they gonna earn any money?

MEN

MINNA ANTRIM (American writer, fl. early 20th c.)
Man forgives woman anything save the wit to outwit him.

BERYL BAINBRIDGE (b. 1934; English novelist and painter)
Quoted in *Picking on Men*:

A man is two people, himself and his cock. A man always takes his friend to the party. Of the two, the friend is nicer, being more able to show his feelings.

CHARLOTTE BINGHAM (b. 1942; English writer)
From *Coronet among the Weeds*:

I can't bear chinless people talking about sex. I think all chinless men should be eunuchs.

NAOMI BLWEIN (20th c. American writer)
Behind almost every woman you ever heard of stands a man who let her down.

ELIZABETH BARRETT BROWNING (1806–61; English poet)
Men get opinions as boys learn to spell,
By reiteration, chiefly.

PHYLLIS DILLER (b. 1917; American comedienne)
On diminutive actor Mickey Rooney:

Mickey Rooney's favourite exercise is climbing tall people.

LESLEY-ANNE DOWN (b. 1957; English actress)
Explaining her unexpected and short-lived marriage to an Argentinian:

Sometimes you fancy egg and chips, sometimes steak and tomatoes.

GEORGE ELIOT (1819–80; English novelist)
From *Adam Bede*:
He was a cock who thought the sun had come to hear him crow.

ZSA ZSA GABOR (b. ?1918; Hungarian-born actress; Miss Hungary 1936; seven times married)
Macho does not prove mucho.

FLORENCE KENNEDY (b. 1916; American feminist writer)
If men could get pregnant, abortion would be a sacrament.

JEAN KERR (b. 1923; American playwright and essaysit)
Women speak because they wish to speak, whereas a man speaks only when driven to speech by something outside himself – like, for instance, he can't find any clean socks.

LYDIA LOPOKOVA (1892–1981; Russian, Diaghilev ballet dancer and wife of economist John Maynard Keynes)
I like to be alone, yes I *do*! But I must have a man for Sunday lunch.

JAYNE MANSFIELD (1932–67; American film actress)
Men are those creatures with two legs and eight arms.

DOROTHY PARKER (1893–1967; American writer, satirist and humorist)
'Chant for Dark Hours'

Some men, some men
Cannot pass a
Book shop.
('Lady, make your mind up, and wait your life away.)

Some men, some men
Cannot pass a

Crap game
(He said he'd come at moonrise, and here's another day!)

Some men, some men
Cannot pass a
Bar-room
(Wait about, and hang about, and that's the way it goes.)

Some men, some men
Cannot pass a
Woman
(Heaven never send me another one of those!)

Some men, some men
Cannot pass a
Golf course.
(Read a book, and sew a seam, and slumber if you can.)

Some men, some men
Cannot pass a
Haberdasher's.
(All your life you wait around for some damn man!)

JOAN RIVERS (b. 1939; American comedienne)

No man ever stuck his hand up your dress looking for a library card.

HELEN ROWLAND (1875–1950; American writer)

The only original thing about some men is original sin.

From *A Guide to Men*:

The average man takes all the natural taste out of his food by covering it with ready-made sauces, and all the personality out of a woman by covering her with his ready-made ideals.

From *A Guide to Men*:

A bachelor never quite gets over the idea that he is a thing of beauty and a boy forever.

From *The Rubaiyat of a Bachelor*:

Never trust a husband too far, nor a bachelor too near.

FRANÇOISE SAGAN (b. 1935; French writer)

I like men to behave like men – strong and childish.

MADAME DE SEVIGNÉ (1626–96; French writer)

I fear nothing so much as a man who is witty all day long.

GERTRUDE STEIN (1874–1946; American writer)

From *Everybody's Autobiography*:

It is funny the two things most men are proudest of is the thing that any man can do and doing does in the same way, that is being drunk and being the father of their son.

GLORIA STEINEM (b. 1934; American feminist writer and co-founder of *Ms.*)

From 'If Men Could Menstruate':

So what would happen if suddenly, magically, men could menstruate and women could not?

Clearly, menstruation would become an enviable, boast-worthy, masculine event:

Men would brag about how long and how much.

Young boys would talk about it as the envied beginning of manhood.

Gifts, religious ceremonies, family dinners, and stag parties would mark the day.

To prevent monthly work loss among the powerful, Congress would fund a National Institute of Dysmenorrhea. Doctors would research little about heart attacks, from which men were hormonally protected, but everything about cramps.

Sanitary supplies would be federally funded and free. Of course, some men would still pay for the prestige of such commercial brands as Paul Newman Tampons, Muhammad Ali's Rope-a-Dope Pads, John Wayne Maxi Pads, and Joe Namath Jock Shields – 'For Those Light Bachelor Days.'

GLORIA SWANSON (1899–1983; American actress)

On Cecil B. de Mille:

He wore baldness like an expensive hat, as if it were out of the question for him to have hair like other men.

MARY AUGUSTA WARD (1851–1920; English writer and social worker)

Every man is bound to leave a story better than he found it.

MAE WEST (1892–1980; American, 'world's greatest movie siren')

Give a man a free hand and he'll try to run it all over you.

I like a man who's good, but not too good. The good die young and I hate a dead one.

A man in the house is worth two on the street.

At forty a man has come of age. He has more polish, charm, poise – and more money.

The guy's no good – he never was any good . . . his mother should have thrown *him* away and kept the stork.

MONEY

NANCY ASTOR (1879–1964; American-born British politician. First woman to take her seat in the House of Commons)

At a political meeting a heckler called out, 'It's all right for you, your husband's a millionaire'. She looked him in the eye and said, 'I should hope he is. That's why I married him!'

JANE AUSTEN (1775–1917; English novelist)

From *Mansfield Park*:

If this man had not twelve thousand a year, he would be a very stupid fellow.

From *Sense and Sensibility*:

People always live for ever where there is any annuity to be paid to them.

PEG BRACKEN (b. 1918; American writer and humorist)

Why does a slight tax increase cost you two hundred dollars and a substantial tax cut save you thirty cents?

MARIA CALLAS (1923–77; American-born, of Greek parents, opera singer)

Maria Callas lived a totally cosmopolitan life. To a New York reporter's question, 'Miss Callas, you were born in the US, brought up in Greece and you sing in Italian. What language do you think in?' she replied, 'I count in English.'

BRITT EKLAND (b. 1942; Swedish film actress)

On rock star Rod Stewart, after the acrimonious break-up of their relationship:

He was so mean, it hurt him to go the bathroom.

DELPHINE DE GIRARDIN (1804–55; French writer)

Business is other people's money.

HETTY GREEN (1834–1916; American multi-millionairess)

Mrs Green was a remarkably shrewd investor and people often hoped to gain useful advice about the stock market from her. For one such hopeful who asked her to name a really good investment she had the following tip: 'The other world.'

NELL GWYNN (1650–87; English actress and mistress of Charles II)

Expensive wars on behalf of his French allies and the constant financial drain of many mistresses and illegitimate children had emptied the King's coffers. When Nell asked him for money he truthfully replied he had none to give.

'Send the French in to France again, set me on the stage again and lock up your own cod-piece,' was her sage advice.

MARGARET CASE HARRIMAN

From *Quotations For Our Time*:

Money is what you'd get on beautifully without if only other people weren't so crazy about it.

KAY INGRAM (20th c. American writer)

Women prefer men who have something tender about them – especially the legal kind.

DOROTHEA JORDAN (1761–1816; English actress and mistress of the Duke of Clarence, later William IV)

Before he became king William IV enjoyed a lengthy relationship with the actress Mrs Jordan, who bore him a large number of children. Parliament constantly criticised the extravagances of William and his brothers and his father persuaded him to cut Mrs Jordan's allowance by a full 50 per cent. She categorically refused to accept this cavalier behaviour, sending him a playbill and drawing his attention to the conditions of sale printed at the bottom, which read: 'No money returned after the rising of the curtain.'

GERTRUDE LAWRENCE (1898–1952; English actress)

Gertrude seldom carried money, and when faced with a $17 purchase in Woolworths told the assistant to 'Charge it'. Amazed to be told by the bemused girl that there were no charge accounts at Woolworths, she asked, 'Then how have you all managed to stay here in business so long?'

MARY MCCOY

Quoted in *Quotations For Our Time*:

The trouble with being a breadwinner nowadays is that the Government is in for such a big slice.

SHIRLEY MACLAINE (b. 1934; American dancer and film actress)

On shopping for bargains in Hong Kong:

Hong Kong was a place where you went broke saving money.

ETHEL WATTS MUMFORD (1878–1940; American writer and humorist)

In the midst of life we are in debt.

DOROTHY PARKER (1893–1967; American writer, satirist and humorist)

The two most beautiful words in the English language are: Cheque Enclosed.

IVY BAKER PRIEST (1905–75; former US Treasurer)

We women ought to put first things first. Why should we mind if men have their faces on the money, as long as we get our hands on it?

GERTRUDE STEIN (1874–1946; American writer)

I do want to get rich but I never want to do what there is to do to get rich.

JULIE WALTERS (b. 1950; English comedy actress)

Talking about adjusting to her new home where she kept bumping into the walls in the dark:

But I know where the bathroom is – that is where I look in the mirror every morning and worry about the mortgage.

CAROLYN WELLS (1869–1942; American humorist and writer)

A fool and his money are soon married.

MAE WEST (1892–1980; American, 'world's greatest movie siren)

On whether her way of getting jewels didn't unnerve her:

No. I was calm and *collected*.

Hollywood gossip columnist Louella Parsons asked her whether she thought she'd be as popular with movie audiences as she had been live on Broadway, where of course the seats cost a lot more:

'Why shouldn't they like me?' replied Mae West. 'Wouldn't you like if it y' were gettin' a Cadillac for the price of a Ford?'

A little hush money can do a lot of talking.

MOVIES

BETTE DAVIS (b. 1908; American film actress)

The best time I ever had with Joan Crawford was when I pushed her down the stairs in *Whatever Happened to Baby Jane?*

MARLENE DIETRICH (b. 1902; German singer and actress)

Refusing to work with any director but Josef von Sternberg:

Von for all and all for Von.

EDNA FERBER (1887–1968; American writer)

Letter to Harold Ross, editor of the *New Yorker*, after the publication of a review of the movie *Classified*, based on a novel by Ferber:

Will you kindly inform the moron who runs your motion picture department that I did not write the movie entitled *Classified*? Neither did I write any of its wisecracking titles. Also inform him that Moses did not write the motion picture entitled *The Ten Commandments*.

JANE FONDA (b. 1937; American actress)

On Laurence Harvey:

Acting with Harvey is like acting by yourself – only worse.

TEXAS GUINAN (1878–1933; American nightclub hostess during Prohibition)

On her early career in over two hundred silent cowboy movies, when she was billed as 'The Female William S. Hart':

We never changed the plots, only the horses.

PEGGY LEE (b. 1920; American singer)

I learned courage from Buddha, Jesus, Lincoln, Einstein and Cary Grant.

CAROLINE LEJEUNE (1897–1973; English film critic and playwright)

In a review of the film *I am a Camera*:

Me no Leica.

MYRNA LOY (b. 1902; American film actress)

On censorship of a love scene in *The Thin Man*:

You should have seen it, with one leg each on the floor we could barely get our lips together. We had to use our necks like turtles – stretching and stretching until we finally got in a little love peck.

FRANCES MARION (1886–1973; American journalist)

We have a little catch phrase in our family which somehow fits almost everyone in the movie colony: 'Spare no expense to make everything as economical as possible.'

DOROTHY PARKER (1893–1967; American writer, satirist and humorist)

Looking out from her window at MGM which overlooked a cemetery she remarked: 'Hello down there. It might interest you to know that up here we are just as dead as you are.'

BARBARA STANWYCK (b. 1907; American actress)

My only problem is finding a way to play my fortieth fallen female in a different way from my thirty-ninth.

ESTHER WILLIAMS (b. 1923; American swimming champion and star of Hollywood swimming extravaganzas)

On her acting career:

I was in the water for only twenty minutes of the two hours. What did they think? Did they think I blew bubbles for the rest of the time?

NAIVETY

TALLULAH BANKHEAD (1902–68; American actress, also known for her outrageous lifestyle)

Having made a large donation to the Salvation Army band which was playing outside her hotel, Tallulah airily refused to be thanked: 'No need, I know what a terrible time it's been lately for you Spanish dancers.'

SARAH BERNHARDT (1844–1923; French tragedienne)

Sarah Bernhardt continued to act although one of her legs had been amputated after an accident on stage. Shortly after the operation she received an offer of $100,000 from the manager of the Pan-American Exposition in San Francisco if he could exhibit her leg. Back came Bernhardt's cable: 'Which leg?'

ELEANOR BRON (b. 1934; English actress)

From *The Pillow Book of Eleanor Bron*:

The greengrocers looked startled when I walked into the shop and saw the pile of new apples, and said, 'How wonderful! It always makes me happy when I see the first Cox of the year.'

EMERALD, LADY CUNARD (née Maud Burke; 1872–1948; American-born British society hostess)

Lady Cunard was one of many wealthy and titled people letting their hair down at a ball to celebrate the end of the Second World War. After watching their exuberant and infantile behaviour for a while the diarist 'Chips' Channon turned to Lady Cunard and remarked in a cynical tone, 'So this is what we fought the war for!'

'Oh,' said Lady Cunard innocently, 'are they all Poles?'

ELAINE DUNDY (b. 1927; American writer)

From *The Dud Avocado*:

I arrived alone at the Ritz, only to discover all over again what a difficult thing this was to do. I tended to lose my balance at the exact moment that the doorman opened the cab door and stood by in his respectful attitude of 'waiting'. I have even been known to fall out of the cab by reaching and pushing against the handle at the same time that he did. But this time, however, I had disciplined myself to remain quite, *quite* still, sitting on my hands until the door was opened for me. Then, burrowing into my handbag, which suddenly looked like the Black Hole of Calcutta, to find the fare, I discovered that I needed a light. A light was switched on. I needed more than a light, I needed a match or a torch or special glasses, for I simply couldn't find my purse, and when I did (lipstick rolling on the floor, compact open and everything spilt – passport, mirror, the works) I couldn't find the right change. We were now all three of us, driver, doorman and I, waiting to see what I was going to do next. I took out some bills, counted them three times in the dark until I was absolutely certain that I had double the amount necessary, and then pressed it on the driver, eagerly apologizing for overtipping. Overcome with shyness I nodded briefly in the direction of the doorman and raced him to the entrance. I just won. Panting and by now in an absolute ecstasy of panic I flung myself at the revolving doors and let them spin me through. Thus I gained access to the Ritz.

DAME EDITH EVANS (1888–1976; English actress)

Commuting by train from Brighton to London, where she was acting in a play with Peggy Ashcroft and Edith Evans, Joyce Carey was deeply distressed by an incident in which a 'flasher' took advantage of the darkness of one of the tunnels to expose himself to her. When she arrived at the theatre Miss Carey was virtually incoherent and when she had told her story Dame Peggy solicitously went in search of brandy for her. Returning to Miss Carey's dressing room she met Dame Edith, who demanded to know *who* was drinking brandy before a matinée.

'It's for Joyce, Edith,' explained Dame Peggy. 'She's had the most dreadful experience.'

Dame Edith then proceeded to Miss Carey's dressing room where the entire story was repeated for her benefit. When Miss Carey had finished Dame Edith paused for a second or two to reflect and then enquired in a voice heavy with sympathy, 'Well, dear, and where exactly *was* this tunnel.'

CONNIE FRANCIS (b. 1938; American singer)

I thought sex was a store on Fifth Avenue . . .

ZSA ZSA GABOR (b. ?1918; Hungarian-born actress; Miss Hungary 1936; seven times married)

When asked how many husbands she had had, she replied, 'You mean apart from my own?'

EDNA O'BRIEN (b. 1932; Irish writer)

'Are you fast?' Baba asked bluntly.
'What's fast?' I interrupted. The word puzzled me.
'It's a woman who has a baby quicker than another woman,' Baba said quickly, impatiently.

LADY REDESDALE (fl. 1900s; English aristocrat, mother of the famous 'Mitford Girls')

One of her daughters, Nancy, who was married to Peter Rodd, a man universally acknowledged as a crashing bore, fell in love with a dashing Free Frenchman during her husband's absence. To her delight she became pregnant, but it was an ectopic pregnancy and in the subsequent operation a hysterectomy was performed. Tearfully Nancy, who had desperately wanted children, reported to 'Muv' (Lady Redesdale) that both her ovaries had been removed.

'Both!' shrieked Lady Redesdale. 'But I thought one had hundreds, like caviar!'

JOAN RIVERS (b. 1939; American comedienne)
From *The Life and Hard Times of Heidi Abromowitz*:

Went to the Vatican today and met the Pope. When he came up to me, I did what everyone else was doing and dropped to my knees. Boy, what a commotion! How the hell did I know it was his ring I was supposed to kiss?

BROOKE SHIELDS (b. 1965; American film actress)

What does 'good in bed' mean to me? When I'm sick and stay home from school propped up with lots of pillows watching TV and my mom brings me soup – that's good in bed.

QUEEN VICTORIA (1819–1901)

From a letter written by the Queen's Lady-in-Waiting, Marie Mallet, 25 March 1899:

The Queen paid a visit to a Zoo Garden near here belonging to a certain Comtesse de la Grange 'ci-devant cocotte' (courtesan), and was presented with a new-laid ostrich egg; this was carefully blown by the chef and its contents manufactured into an omelette which Her Majesty pronounced delicious. On the egg the doubtful Comtesse had scrawled her name, 'Just as if she had laid it herself' remarked the Queen quite naively!

MAE WEST (1892–1980; American, 'world's greatest movie siren')

Asked by her screen lover if he could trust her, she said, 'You can. Hundreds have.'

OPTIMISM

TALLULAH BANKHEAD (1902–68; American actress, also known for her outrageous lifestyle)

Cocaine isn't habit-forming. I should know – I've been using it for years.

CORAL BROWNE (b. 1913; Australian-born actress)

Having been cast in a production of King Lear Miss Browne was anxious that a part be found for her husband so that they could tour together. Although there were no obvious parts for which he was suitable she refused to be beaten. Poring over the text she turned, vindicated, to the director and pointed to the stage direction: *'A Camp Near Dover.'*

PAULINE DANIELS (b. 1955; English comic on the Northern Clubs circuit)

I still like a man to open a door for me – even if he does let it swing back and hit me in the face.

SHELAGH DELANEY (b. 1939; Irish playwright)

From *A Taste of Honey*:

The only consolation I can find in your immediate presence is your ultimate absence.

PHYLLIS DILLER (b. 1917; American comedienne)

On the occasion of a dinner to honour veteran George Burns: You don't know what a thrill this is for me to be here with George Burns. I've had a crush on George for years. He's my kind of guy. He's handsome . . . he's successful . . . and he's breathing.

LYDIA LOPOKOVA (1892–1981; Russian, Diaghilev ballet dancer and wife of economist John Maynard Keynes; often deliberately misused English to comic effect)

When her Russian divorce came through she was delighted: 'Thank God, I am a virgin again.'

PHYLLIS MCGINLEY (1905–78; American writer and essayist)

From 'Song Against Sweetness and Light':

O merry is the Optimist,
With the troops of courage leaguing.
But a dour trend
In any friend
Is somehow less fatiguing.

ADAH ISAACS MENKEN (1835–68; American actress and dancer)

On Lola Montez (a contemporary courtesan);

Lola Montez began with a king and ran down the scale through a newspaper man to a miner; I began with a prize-fighter, and I will end with a prince.

DOROTHY PARKER (1893–1967; American writer, satirist and humorist)

From a review of one of Margot Asquith's over-long books in her column in the *New Yorker*:

'Daddy, what's an optimist?' said Pat to Mike while they were walking down the street together one day.

'One who thought that Margot Asquith wasn't going to write any more,' replied the absent-minded professor, as he wound up the cat and put the clock out.

MOLLY PICON (b. 1898; Jewish-American actress)

When some of the company with which she was touring complained about their accommodation Miss Picon remarked, 'You won't hear *me* complain – my grandmother raised eleven children in just four rooms.'

'However did she manage?' asked one of the company.

'No problem,' came the reply. 'She took in lodgers.'

MAE WEST (1892–1980; American, 'world's greatest movie siren')

I feel like a million tonight – but one at a time.

PESSIMISM

BINNIE BARNES (b. 1906; English actress)

He's the kind of bore who's here today and here tomorrow.

DJUNA BARNES (1892–1982; American writer)

From 'The Jest of Jests':

There are no pitfalls for the woman over forty . . . There's only one possibility for her, and that is she will end life on a sofa with hot bottles at head and feet.

SARAH BERNHARDT (1844–1923; French tragedienne)

In her heyday Sarah Bernhardt was strikingly attractive and had many admirers. When she was old one of these former suitors came to visit her in her Paris apartment at the very top of a tall block. Out of breath after his climb her friend asked why she continued to live up so many flights of stairs.

'Nowadays,' came the reply, 'it is the only way I am still able to make men's hearts beat a little faster.'

CHARLOTTE BINGHAM (b. 1942; English writer)

A twenty-five-year-old virgin is like the man set upon by thieves: everyone passes by.

STEPHANIE CALMAN (b. 1960; English writer)

On a visit to a particularly sleazy nightclub (from *Gentlemen Prefer My Sister*):

The sight of a waitress here is so rare, they give you a pack of distress flares at the door.

LADY DIANA COOPER (1892–1986; English socialite)

The Coopers were staying with the Guinnesses on their new yacht which was not yet named. Several possible names were discussed, including Gloria Mundi in honour of their hostess, Gloria.

'Sick Transit might be better,' was Lady Diana's opinion.

PHYLLIS DILLER (b. 1917; American comedienne)

When asked by Society Photographer Allen Warren why she wished to be photographed with a telephone in her hand she answered, wryly, 'Because I'm Phyllis Diller, the only lady who receives dirty phone calls collect!'

ANN FLEMING (b. 1913; wife of the novelist Ian Fleming)

Last night I would have put my head in the gas oven, if I was not too frightened of the cook to go into the kitchen.

RACHEL HEYHOE FLINT (b. 1937; former England women's cricket captain)

After being dropped as captain of the England Women's Cricket Team:

As one door closes another slams in your face.

DAME MADGE KENDAL (1849–1945; English actress)

Commenting on the work of birth control pioneer Marie Stopes:

Sister Susie built her hopes

On the books of Marie Stopes.
But I fear from her condition,
She must have read the wrong edition.

FLORENCE KING (b. 1936; American writer and critic)
From *Confessions of a Failed Southern Lady*:

The waitress spread newspapers over [the table] and we ordered a mess of softshell. When they came, we all fell to except Evelyn, who was staring at an empty pickle jar on the table.

'I'm going to steal that jar,' she whispered.

'Why?' asked Charlotte. 'There's nothing in it except juice.'

'I know, that's why I want it. It's *pickle* juice.'

She rolled her popping eyes around the room to make sure no one was watching; then she grabbed the jar, screwed the lid tight, and shoved it in her big straw handbag.

'It's so's I can catch my womb in case it falls out,' she informed us.

FELICIA LAMPORT (American writer)
From *Scrap Irony*:

> The after-effects of a mother's neglects,
> May spoil her boy's orientation to sex.
> But the converse is worse: if she over-protects,
> The pattern of Oedipus wrecks.

AMY LOWELL (1874–1925; American poet and critic)
Amy Lowell had an intense dislike of the Cabot family, who regarded themselves as superior because they were one of the oldest families in Boston. Wherever possible she avoided any occasion where any of them might be present. About to set out across the Atlantic for a trip to Europe she disembarked at the last minute, having read the passenger list. Asked why she had changed her mind she replied: 'There are sixteen Cabots aboard that ship and God is unlikely to forego such a wonderful opportunity.'

DOROTHY PARKER (1893–1967; American writer, satirist and humorist)

Take me or leave me; or, as is the usual order of things, both.

From 'Wallflower's Lament':

It has lately been drawn to your correspondent's attention that, at social gatherings, she is not the human magnet she would be. Indeed, it turns out that as a source of entertainment, conviviality, and good fun, she ranks somewhere between a sprig of parsley and a single ice-skate.

LETTY COTTIN POGREBIN (b. 1939; American writer and journalist)

Boys don't make passes at female smart-asses.

JOAN RIVERS (b. 1939; American comedienne)

From *The Life and Hard Times of Heidi Abromowitz*:

Her [Heidi's] bra size was the same as her IQ – 40. I was so flat I used to put x's on my chest and write, 'You are here.' (For a while I considered having 'Play other side' tattooed on my back.) I wore angora sweaters just so the guys would have *something* to pet.

HELEN ROWLAND (1875–1950; American writer)

A bachelor who has passed forty is a remnant; there is no good material in him.

LADY MARY WILSON (English, wife of former Labour Prime Minister Sir Harold Wilson)

After Harold Wilson, as Leader of the Labour Party, won the 1964 General Election and became Prime Minister, Mrs Wilson, as she then was, observed that 'Of course, there is nowhere to hang out washing in Downing Street.'

PHILOSOPHY

JANE ACE (1905–74; American radio comedienne and actress)

Time wounds all heels.

NANCY ASTOR (1879–1964; American-born British politician. First woman to take her seat in the House of Commons)

On being a staunch teetotaller:

One reason I don't drink is that I want to know when I'm having a good time.

TALLULAH BANKHEAD (1902–68; American actress, also known for her outrageous lifestyle)

I'm the foe of moderation, the champion of excess.

ELIZABETH BOWEN (1899–1973; Anglo-Irish writer)

Meeting people unlike oneself does not enlarge one's outlook; it only confirms one's idea that one is unique.

EDNA FERBER (1887–1968; American writer)

From *Roast Beef Medium*:

Roast Beef, Medium, is not only a food. It is a philosophy. Seated at Life's Dining Table, with the menu of Morals before you, your eye wanders a bit over the entrées, the hors d'oeuvres, and the things *à la* though you know that Roast Beef, Medium, is safe and sane, and sure.

MRS GASKELL (1810–65; English novelist)

I'll not listen to reason . . . Reason always means what someone else has got to say.

ELLEN GLASGOW (1874–1945; American writer)

The only difference between a rut and a grave is their dimensions.

THE HON MRS RONALD GREVILLE (d. 1942; fashionable society hostess; daughter of wealthy Scottish brewer McEwan)

I would rather be a beeress than a peeress.

ALICE ROOSEVELT LONGWORTH (1884–1980; American, daughter of President Theodore Roosevelt; nicknamed 'Princess Malice')

I have a simple philosophy. Fill what's empty. Empty what's full. And scratch where it itches.

PHYLLIS MCGINLEY (1905–78; American writer and essayist)

> 'Lament for a Wavering Viewpoint'
>
> Ah, snug lie those that slumber
> Beneath Conviction's roof.
> Their floors are sturdy lumber,
> Their windows weather-proof.
> But I sleep cold forever
> And cold sleep all my kind,
> For I was born to shiver
> In the draft from an open mind.

BETTE MIDLER (b. 1945; American actress, comedienne and singer)

Being moral isn't what you *do*, . . . it's what you *mean* to do.

FLORENCE NIGHTINGALE (1820–1910; English nurse in Crimean War)

I am not at all of Socrates' opinion that it is better to perish by other people's folly. I think nothing is so provoking.

MOLLY PARKIN (b. 1932; English comedienne, actress and writer)

I like the *philosophy* of the sandwich, as it were. It typifies my attitude to life, really. It's all there, it's fun, it looks good, and you don't have to wash up afterwards.

DIANE DE POITIERS (1499–1566; mistress of Henry II of France)

For a good enemy, choose a friend. He knows where to strike.

STEVIE SMITH (1902–71; English poet)

> 'On the Death of a German Philosopher'
>
> He wrote The I and the It
> He wrote The It and Me
> He died at Marienbad
> And now we are all at sea.

JANE TAYLOR (1783–1824; English writer)

> Though man a thinking being is defined,
> Few use the grand prerogative of mind.
> How few think justly of the thinking few!
> How many never think, who think they do.

MAE WEST (1892–1980; American, 'world's greatest movie siren')

Between two evils, I always pick the one I never tried before.

Don't let any guy put anything over on ya – except an umbrella.

POLITICS

BELLA ABZUG (b. 1920; American lawyer and Congresswoman)

Richard Nixon self-impeached himself. He gave us Gerald Ford as his revenge.

SUSAN B. ANTHONY (1820–1906; pioneer American feminist and temperance campaigner)

Samuel May, himself a campaigner against slavery, mocked her feminist stance, saying that an unmarried woman had no business discussing marriage.

'Mr May,' was her reply, 'If you are not a slave why are you campaigning against slavery?'

NANCY ASTOR (1879–1964; American-born British politician; first woman to take her seat in the House of Commons)

When a group of MPs were muttering that they didn't know what to make of their ambitious and troublesome fellow MP Winston Churchill, Nancy Astor replied sweetly: 'Why not a nice rug?'

LADY VIOLET BONHAM CARTER (1887–1969; English Liberal politician)

Comparing David Lloyd George with Andrew Bonar Law:

We have to choose between one man suffering from St Vitus's Dance and another from sleeping sickness.

LADY CLARISSSA EDEN (b. 1920; wife of former Prime Minister Sir Anthony Eden)

At the time of the Suez Crisis in 1956:

During the last few weeks I have felt that the Suez Canal was flowing through my drawing room.

HERMIONE GINGOLD (b. 1897; English actress and comedienne)

There are too many men in politics and not enough elsewhere.

TEXAS GUINAN (1878–1933; American nightclub hostess during Prohibition)

A politician is a fellow who will lay down your life for his country.

FRANCES HUTT (1903–70; wife of American politician Thomas Dewey)

In 1948 it seemed that Dewey might be successful against Harry S. Truman in the presidential election. As the votes started coming in the excited Dewey asked his wife, 'How do you like the idea of sleeping with the President of the United States?'

'Of course it would be an honour,' was her reply, 'and one I can hardly wait to enjoy.'

The next morning Dewey's high hopes were proved unfounded and Truman was re-elected President.

'Well, darling,' said Mrs Dewey to her despondent husband, 'Will Harry be coming here or do I have to go to Washington?'

FELICITY KENDAL (b. 1946; English actress)

There's one sure way of telling when politicians aren't telling the truth – their lips move.

ALICE ROOSEVELT LONGWORTH (1884–1980; American, daughter of President Theodore Roosevelt; nicknamed 'Princess Malice')

Even after her father's death, Alice regarded all other presidents and presidential candidates as hated rivals. Her cousin Franklin, who was married to the formidable Eleanor, she described uncharitably as: 'One-third sap, two-thirds Eleanor.'

Of Thomas Dewey, the Republican candidate beaten in two successive presidential elections, she was scathing: 'You can't make a soufflé rise twice.'

CLARE BOOTHE LUCE (b. 1903; American writer, politician and diplomat)

In politics women type the letters, lick the stamps, distribute the pamphlets and get out the vote. Men get elected.

ROSA LUXEMBURG (1870–1919; German Marxist revolutionary)

On herself, at the outbreak of the First World War:

There are only two *men* left in the party – Klara Zetkin and I.

PHYLLIS MCGINLEY (1905–78; American writer and essayist)

'Ballad of the Preelection Vote'

No candidate too pallid,
No issue too remote,
But it can snare
A questionnaire

112

To analyze our vote.

GOLDA MEIR (1898–1978; Israeli Prime Minister)

Under President Nixon the US Secretary of State was Henry Kissinger, a German-born lawyer who retained his heavy accent despite many years in America. At a meeting between Mrs Meir and Nixon the President remarked that now they both had Jewish foreign ministers. 'Yes,' agreed Mrs Meir, 'but mine speaks English.'

VIRGILIA PETERSON (1904–66; American writer and TV personality)

Perhaps it is the expediency in the political eye that blinds it.

ELEANOR ROOSEVELT (1884–1962; American writer and humanitarian, wife of President Franklin D. Roosevelt)

Speech before the Democratic National Convention, Chicago, 23 July 1952:

There is a small articulate minority in this country which advocates changing our national symbol, which is the eagle, to that of the ostrich and withdrawing from the UN.

ADELA ROGERS ST JOHNS (b. 1894; American journalist and writer)

Why keep the [Watergate] tapes around? It's like you left the corpse in the bullring.

PAT SHROEDER (contemporary American Congresswoman)
On President Reagan:

He has achieved a political breakthrough – the Teflon-coated presidency. He sees to it that nothing sticks to him.

ELIZABETH CADY STANTON (1815–1902; American suffragette and writer)

On her frustration at the slow progress of women's emancipation: I am at a boiling point! If I do not find some day the use of my tongue on this question I shall die of an intellectual repression, a woman's rights convulsion.

GLORIA STEINEM (b. 1934; American feminist writer, and co-founder of *Ms*.)
Referring to the security problem posed by the Watergate crisis:
When Nixon is alone in a room, is there anyone there?

MARGARET THATCHER (b. 1925; English politician, first female Prime Minister)
In politics, if you want anything said, ask a man; if you want anything done, ask a woman.

To former Labour Prime Minister James Callaghan's back-handed compliment, 'May I congratulate you on being the only man in your team?' she replied tartly, 'That's one more than you've got in yours!'

QUEEN VICTORIA (1819–1901)
On crusading Liberal Prime Minister William Gladstone:
He speaks to me as if I was a public meeting.

MAE WEST (1892–1980; American, 'world's greatest movie siren')
I've always had a weakness for foreign affairs.

I don't know a lot about politics, but I know a good party man when I see one.

DAME REBECCA WEST (1892–1983; English novelist and critic)
To Winston Churchill, after they had both listened to a dreary speech by a politician:
Now I can say with perfect truth that you and I have slept together.

Margaret Thatcher has one great advantage . . . she is a daughter of the people and looks trim . . . Shirley Williams has such an advantage over her because she's a member of the upper middle class and can achieve the kitchen-sink-revolutionary look that one cannot get unless one has been to a really good school.

SHIRLEY WILLIAMS (b. 1930; English politician)
On the House of Commons:
It's not so much a gentleman's club as a boys' boarding school.

QUICK THINKING

LOUISA MAY ALCOTT (1832–88; American writer)
The success of her books made Louisa May Alcott a sought-after public figure, which was not entirely to her liking. On one occasion an overpowering matron struggled through the crowd to take her hand and enthuse, 'If you ever come to Oshkosh your feet will not be allowed to touch the ground: you will be borne in the arms of the people. Will you come?'

'Never,' was Miss Alcott's firm and immediate response.

MADELINE TALMADGE ASTOR (fl. 1890–1945; American society hostess)
[Attributed, as she was helped over the rail of the Titanic]
I rang for ice, but *this* is ridiculous!

TALLULAH BANKHEAD (1902–68; American actress, also known for her outrageous lifestyle)
When, in the spirit of objective scientific inquiry, Dr Alfred Kinsey, the pioneer sex therapist, asked Tallulah to tell him all about her sex life (which had been wild, excessive and exhibitionist), she countered: 'Naturally, but you must tell me all about yours first.'

Actor Donald Sutherland was making up alone in his dressing room. Suddenly he turned round and there was Tallulah Bankhead standing stark naked in the doorway.

'What's the matter, dahling,' drawled Tallulah, seeing his look of amazement, 'haven't you ever seen a blonde before?'

A young woman paying a visit to the lavatory was amazed to hear Tallulah's unmistakable gravelly tones coming from the neighbouring cubicle.

'Say, there's no paper in here, do you have any in there with you?'

Receiving a negative reply she tried again, 'Well, do you have any Kleenex on you?'

Again, the reply was negative.

'Not even some cotton wool or a piece of wrapping paper?'

A long pause followed the third negative, then there was the sound of a purse opening and a resigned voice came through the partition, 'Would you have two fives for a ten?'

LILIAN BAYLIS (1874–1937; English music-hall singer and founder of the Old Vic)

Lilian Baylis was hit by a car while crossing the road with a friend. When help finally arrived her friend, thinking he might get everyone to respond a little faster, exclaimed, 'Don't you know who this is? It's Lilian Baylis of the Old Vic.'

At which point the hitherto unconscious Miss Baylis lifted her head, asserted firmly, 'And of Sadler's Wells,' and fell back on to the road.

DAME CLARA BUTT (1873–1936; English singer)

Lord Rhondda, who survived the sinking of the *Lusitania* during the First World War, found this cable from Dame Clara waiting for him on his return to dry land:

Congratulations on your lucky escape. Will you give me £1000 for the Prince of Wales's box at my Red Cross concert?

MRS PATRICK CAMPBELL (1865–1940; English actress)

When she was presented to Kaiser William II he complimented her on her gentle voice (at a time when she had a severe cold and could hardly speak in more than a whisper). 'You must come again, if only to teach my actors not to bellow,' said the Kaiser.

'I wish, sir, that I *could* bellow,' she replied.

* * *

'Who's responsible for this?' demanded an irate New York taxi driver, discovering a puddle on the floor of his cab.

'I am,' replied Mrs Campbell grandly, alighting from the taxi with her dog.

PATRICIA COCKBURN (b. 1914; Irish travel writer and journalist)

Quoting her mother, who discovered their butler lying dead drunk under the dining table just before a big dinner party:

Stay where you are, Jones, and don't touch any of the ladies' ankles.

DAME GLADYS COOPER (1888–1971; English actress)

Driving through America in the 1950s, Dame Gladys made a 'comfort stop' at a motel, only to discover it had been entirely taken over by the General Motors annual dinner.

Non-car-workers were being turned away. Undeterred she sent for the head waiter and said:

'You won't know me, but I'm an old English actress and I happen to be a great friend of the General's, who would like me to eat here.'

DIANA DORS (1931–84; English actress)

At a dinner given for Diana Dors, one of her admirers, an actor, proposed a toast to her, saying, 'I cannot claim to know Miss Dors well but I should like to – and when we met this evening she gave me the eye and I could hear her saying to herself, "There's the man I'd like to be made love to by." '

Miss Dors rose and replied, 'I protest at what the speaker has just said. He knows perfectly well that, even when talking to myself, I should never end a sentence with two prepositions.'

QUEEN ELIZABETH II (b. 1926)

When Sir Stanley Rous asked her whether she thought anyone had played well in a particularly dull football Cup Final, the Queen replied as she left, 'Yes, the band.'

MARY GARDEN (1877–1967; Scottish/American opera singer)

When Chauncey Depew asked what was holding up her daringly low-cut gown she smiled sweetly and murmured, 'Your age and my discretion.'

PAULETTE GODDARD (b. 1911; American film actress)

A would-be suitor wanted to know her favourite flowers. 'Tell the idiot I adore white violets,' she replied. 'He'll never find any, so I won't have to bother to thank him.'

RUTH GORDON (1896–1984; American actress)

From *Over Twenty-One*:

Max: Say, is it too early for a drink?
Polly: What's early about it? It's tomorrow in Europe and yesterday in China.

NELL GWYNN (1650–87; English actress and mistress of Charles II)

When a hostile crowd mistook her carriage for that of the King's French Catholic mistress she averted the danger by putting her head out of the window and bawling, 'Pray, good people, be civil, I am the *Protestant* whore.'

JUDY HOLLIDAY (1923–65; American actress)

Miss Holliday went for an audition with a Hollywood movie mogul. True to stereotype he began to pursue her around the desk in a bid to get her on to the 'casting couch'. As he began to gain on her she drew to a halt, put her hands down the front of her dress and with admirable aplomb presented him with her falsies, saying, 'Here, I think these are what you are after.'

FLORYNCE KENNEDY (b. 1916; American feminist writer)

To a male heckler who called out, 'Are you a lesbian?' she swiftly retorted, 'Are you my alternative?'

BEATRICE LILLIE (LADY PEEL) (b. 1898; Canadian-born comedy actress)

A mortified waiter spilt soup over her at a Buckingham Palace dinner party. 'Never darken my Dior again!' she quipped.

ANITA LOOS (1888–1981; American novelist and screen writer)

In the 1960s, Anita Loos visited 'swinging' London. During a televised interview she was asked whether, in view of the changes taking place in society she would have chosen a different theme for her 1920s novel, *Gentlemen Prefer Blondes*. Without hesitation Miss Loos replied, 'Gentlemen Prefer Gentlemen.'

MARILYN MONROE (1926–62; American actress)

After the famous nude calendar was published a reporter asked Marilyn Monroe, 'Did you really have nothing on when you posed for those pictures?'

'Oh, yes,' smiled Marilyn, 'I had the radio on.'

DOROTHY PARKER (1893–1967; American writer, satirist and humorist)

When asked to make a sentence including the word 'horticulture':

You can lead a horticulture but you can't make her think.

To Harold Ross, editor of the *New Yorker*, when he asked her why she had not been in to the office to write an article which was long overdue:

Someone was using the pencil.

LOUISE SIEFF (contemporary member of the Sieff family which runs the English retail chain, Marks and Spencer)

Interior decorator Michael Grimwade relates the following incident, which took place when he was helping Ms Sieff to redecorate her London house. In search of blinds of exactly the required shade, they were on the point of entering the Sloane Square department store, Peter Jones, when a half-used, somewhat oily pack of butter thudded on to the pavement at their feet, completely out of the blue. Without pausing, Ms Sieff stepped over it and entered the shop, remarking, 'I see Marlon Brando's in town.'

MARGARET THATCHER (b. 1925; English politician, first female Prime Minister)

After she had been drunkenly propositioned at Holyrood House, she neatly countered, 'You have very good taste. But I don't think you would make it at the moment.'

MAE WEST (1892–1980; American, 'world's greatest movie siren')

On Rex Reed, a co-star in *Myra Breckenridge*, who criticized both the film and her acting:

That son of a bitch! I oughta get some tough guys to break his legs! No, I got a better idea. He's a writer. I'll have them break his fingers.

EDITH WHARTON (1862–1937; American writer)

Miss Wharton was understandably proud of her beautiful Massachusetts home, The Mount, and agreed to let a rather patronizing French connoisseur visit it and see its treasures. As he left he condescendingly let her know he approved of everything except the bas-relief in the hall. With deceptive politeness the novelist responded: 'I can assure you you will never see it again.'

RELIGION

SOPHIE ARNOULD (1740–1902; French opera singer)

Women give themselves to God when the devil wants nothing more to do with them.

NANCY ASTOR (1879–1964; American-born British politician. First woman to take her seat in the House of Commons)

General Montgomery, on meeting her, said, 'Lady Astor, I must tell you I don't approve of women politicians.'

To which Nancy Astor replied, 'That's all right – the only general I approve of is Evangeline Booth.' [a female officer in the Salvation Army]

HELEN OLCOTT BELL (1830–1918; American writer)

To a woman, the consciousness of being well-dressed gives a sense of tranquillity which religion fails to bestow.

CATHERINE BRAMWELL-BOOTH (b. 1883; English, granddaughter of the founder of the Salvation Army)

On her value as a member of the Salvation Army:

Lord help me. I can love thee and love sinners more, but that's all I can do. The others are better at talking and singing solo.

LADY DIANA COOPER (1892–1986; English socialite)

When asked why, when saying the Lord's Prayer, she left out the phrase, 'And lead us not into temptation,' she replied, 'It's no business of His.'

MARIE ANNE, MARQUISE DU DEFFAND (1697–1780; French society intellectual)

The Marquise was famous for her salon which attracted all the greatest intellectuals of the day. At one of these she was cornered by the Cardinal de Polignac, who insisted on telling her the story of the martyrdom of St Denis, who carried his decapitated head to the area of Paris now named after him. Sensing the Marquise's boredom and possible disbelief the clergyman demanded, 'Do you deny he carried his head a full league?'

'Oh, no,' replied the Marquise, 'I only question the first step.'

PHYLLIS DILLER (b. 1917; American comedienne)

A sixty-two-year-old friend of mine went to bed at night and prayed, 'Please, God, give me skin like a teenager's.' Next day she woke up with pimples.

DAME EDITH EVANS (1888–1976; English actress)

Dr Billy Graham, the American evangelist, met Dame Edith and flattered her by saying how much those in the religious ministry could learn from actors about putting their message across.

'Ah, but you have the advantage over us,' responded Dame Edith. 'In the ministry you have long-term contracts.'

WILLA GIBBS (American writer)
From *The Dean*:
The three kinds of services you generally find in the Episcopal Churches. I call them either low and lazy, broad and hazy, or high and crazy.

ANN KENNARD (former Personnel Chief for the New York City Health Dept)
On being asked if she believed in reincarnation:
Indeed yes. I witness a demonstration every day at five o'clock, when dead employees come to life in time to go home.

FLORENCE KING (b. 1926; American writer and critic)
From *Confessions of a Failed Southern Lady*:
'Girls in occupied countries always get in trouble with soldiers,' [said my grandmother] when I asked her what the Virgin birth was.

DUCHESSE DE LUYNES (fl. 1890s; French wit and socialite)
After hearing a religious fanatic insist that the Virgin Mary came to his room every night:
'Well, he's luckier than Joseph was!'

MIRIAM MARGOYLES (b. ?1944; English actress)
I'm not really a practising Jew, but I keep a kosher kitchen just to spite Hitler.

LAURA RIDING (b. 1901; American poet and writer)
I met God.
  'What,' he said, 'you already?'
  'What,' I said, 'you still?'

ELIZABETH CADY STANTON (1815–1902; American suffragette and writer)

I asked them why . . . one read in the synagogue service every week the 'I thank thee, O Lord, that I was not born a woman.' '. . . It is not meant in an unfriendly spirit, and it is not intended to degrade or humiliate women.' 'But it does, nevertheless. Suppose the service read, "I thank thee, O Lord, that I was not born a jackass." Could that be twisted in any way into a compliment to the jackass?'

MRS ROBERT A. TAFT (born Martha Wheaton Bowers; 1891–1958; wife of US Presidential candidate Robert Alphonso Taft)

I always find that statistics are hard to swallow and impossible to digest. The only one I can ever remember is that if all the people who go to sleep in church were laid end to end they would be a lot more comfortable.

ANGELA THIRKELL (1890–1961; English novelist)

'Indeed the times are troubled,' he said, 'but we must remember that we are all in God's hands.'
'I know we are,' said Mrs Brandon earnestly, laying her hand on the vicar's sleeve, 'and that is what is so *dreadful*.'

IRENE THOMAS (b. 1920; English writer and broadcaster)

Protestant women may take the pill. Roman Catholic women must keep taking the Tablet.

MICHELENE WANDOR (b. 1940; English writer)

Jewish mother to her daughter (from *Guests in the Body*):

'You got to become a lesbian, you should at least have the decency to shack up with a nice Jewish girl.'

MAE WEST (1892–1980; American, 'world's greatest movie siren')

Moral Rearmament is just what Bill [W.C. Fields] needs. Give it to him in a bottle and he'll go for it.

MARGOT ASQUITH (1868–1945; English socialite and political hostess, wife of Prime Minister Herbert Asquith)

Of Lord Hugh Cecil:

I saw him riding in the Row, clinging to his horse like a string of onions.

CHARLOTTE BINGHAM (b. 1942; English writer)

Everyone in advertising is ex-something. Ex-actors, ex-artists, ex-writers, and quite a few ex-people too.

CORAL BROWNE (b. 1913; Australian-born actress)

At the Caprice restaurant, much patronised by theatre folk, Coral Brown spied Radie Harris, theatrical critic of the *Hollywood Reporter*. Miss Harris was a distinguished journalist in her field, but one not much rated by Miss Browne. However, nobody could deny that she was a brave and courageous woman. She had had one leg amputated after an accident, but managed remarkably well with a wooden leg. Seeing Radie surrounded by a sycophantic group of young actors, all paying court to her in the hope of attaining a favourable mention, Coral Browne was heard to exclaim: 'Look at poor Radie Harris, with the whole world at her foot.'

ANITA BRYANT (b. 1940; American anti-gay campaigner)

If homosexuality were the normal way God would have made Adam and Bruce.

MRS PATRICK CAMPBELL (1865–1940; English actress)

To a visitor who admired her frilly lampshades:

Oh, do you like them? I cut up my drawers.

At one of the many dinners given in her honour in America she found herself seated next to an insectologist whose ruling passion was the life-style of the ant, and who seemed unable to talk on any other topic.

'They are such fascinating creatures,' he told her. 'They have a properly organised system, with its own rulers and workers. They even have their own police force and army . . .'

Unable to cope any longer Mrs Pat affected a dead-pan expression and in an intense whisper asked, 'Do they have a navy too?'

COLETTE (1873–1954; French novelist)

The only really masterful noise a man ever makes in a house is the noise of his key, when he is still on the landing, fumbling for the lock.

MARGARET FULLER (1810–50; American writer and philosopher)

Margaret Fuller met the wife of Presidential candidate Horace Greeley while out walking. Mrs Greeley looked at her kid gloves and said disdainfully, 'Ugh, skin of a beast.'

'And what do you wear?' enquired Margaret Fuller politely.

'Silk, of course.'

'Entrails of a worm,' responded Miss Fuller equally fastidiously.

AVA GARDNER (b. 1922; American actress)

On Clark Gable, star of films such as *Gone With the Wind*, and better known for his startling good looks than his sparkling intellect:

If you say 'Hiya, Clark, how are you?' he's stuck for an answer.

MARTHA GELLHORN (b. 1908; American writer)

In a letter to her friend Lady Diana Cooper, who had a reputation for hypochondria as a young girl – and who is now in her nineties! (quoted in *Diana Cooper* by Philip Ziegler):

If I hadn't heard you were safely back at Chantilly, I would be frantic for fear you were dead as a smelt. Have all the pains and anguishes gone? Was it anything like the year you decided your heart was weak or the year you had cancer? It's awful to enjoy your ailments as much as I do, but they've always been so wonderful, so fatal and so sad that I cannot help liking them.

TEXAS GUINAN (1878–1933; American nightclub hostess during Prohibition)
On an unnamed admirer:
He brought me so many orchids that I looked like a well-kept grave.

LILLIAN HELLMAN (1905–84; American playwright and writer)
A number of highly successful American men were sent a magazine questionnaire which included the question, 'During which activity, moment or situation do you feel most masculine?' Pleased with the response to their questionnaire and with its results the magazine decided to send it to a selected number of high-achieving women. Lillian Hellman received the questionnaire and her answer to that particular question was: 'I feel at my most masculine when I write to tell you I do not answer questions like these unless I am paid to do so.'

ALICE ROOSEVELT LONGWORTH (1884–1980; American, daughter of President Theodore Roosevelt; nicknamed 'Princess Malice')
On her cousin, Eleanor Roosevelt, wife of President Franklin D. Roosevelt, and much admired for her good works:
She was too noble – a person who had gone down in one coal mine too many.

CAITLIN MACNAMARA (b. 1913; wife of Welsh poet Dylan Thomas)
To the painter Dod Proctor, who announced she was going to powder her nose:
Why don't you put it in a bag?

KITTY MUGGERIDGE (b, ?1905; English writer, wife of Malcolm Muggeridge)
Of over-confident TV star David Frost:
He has risen without trace.

YOKO ONO (b. 1933; Japanese poet and painter; widow of John Lennon)

I wonder why men can get serious at all. They have this delicate long thing hanging outside their bodies, which goes up and down by its own will . . . If I were a man I would always be laughing at myself.

DOROTHY PARKER (1893–1967; American writer, satirist and humorist)

He [co-writer Robert Benchley] and I had an office so thin that an inch smaller and it would have been adultery.

During one of the famous Round Table lunches at the Algonquin Dorothy Parker rose saying, 'Excuse me, I have to go to the bathroom.'

    After a brief pause she continued, 'Actually I want to make a telephone call but I'm too embarrassed to tell you.'

CORA PEARL (d. 1886; wealthy English courtesan in Paris)

In reply to a young suitor who had written to her, 'Command me and I will die':

I would rather you lived and paid my bills!

JOAN RIVERS (b. 1939; American comedienne)

Madonna is so hairy, when she lifted up her arm I thought it was Tina Turner in her arm-pit.

CATHERINE SEDLEY, COUNTESS OF DORCHESTER (1657–1717)

The Countess was undeniably attractive, although it was her vivacious personality not her appearance (she had a cast in one eye) which accounted for her success with men. She was the mistress of James II who seemed bewitched by her. Trying to analayse why the King was so enthralled by her, she said: 'It cannot be my beauty, for he must see I have none, and it cannot be my wit, for he has not enough to know I have any.'

MERIDEL LE SUEUR (b. 1900; American historian, writer and poet)

Memory in America suffers amnesia.

MAE WEST (1892–1980; American, 'world's greatest movie siren')

Personally, the only good woman I can recall in history was Betsy Ross [designer of the 'Stars and Stripes'], and all she ever made was a flag.

Asked whether she was showing contempt for the Court:

No, I'm trying to hide it.

ROYALTY

PRINCESS ANNE (b. 1950)

When I'm approaching a water jump with fifty or sixty photographers clicking away, television cameras zooming in to catch me going in head first and a couple of thousand spectators swarming all over the place, the only one who doesn't know I'm royal is the horse.

To an over-familiar reporter on one of her trips to America:

I'm not your love, I'm Your Royal Highness.

MARGUERITE, COUNTESS OF BLESSINGTON (1789–1849; English writer and socialite)

Between his many and various attempts to claim the French throne the Emperor Napoleon III took refuge in England where he was glad to accept Lady Blessington's hospitality and to attend her literary salon. However, when she in her turn sought refuge in France from debt and scandal Napoleon, frightened that her notorious reputation might damage his current position as President of the Republic, pointedly ignored her. Eventually they came face to face and Napoleon was forced into conversation.

'Will you be staying long in France, Lady Blessington?' he

asked her, correctly but coldly.

Equally correct, she answered in the affirmative, and then enquired equally coldly, 'And what about you?'

QUEEN ELIZABETH I (1533–1603)

John Aubrey in his *Brief Lives* tells the following tale of royal malice:

Edward de Vere, an assiduous courtier of Elizabeth I, was so deeply distressed to have farted while executing a low and obsequious bow that he immediately put himself into voluntary exile for a period of seven years. When the time had come when he felt the incident must surely have been forgotten he returned to England's shores and hurried to re-present himself at Court. He received a friendly welcome, but as he bowed low once again in obeisance to his sovereign she was unable to refrain from remarking graciously: 'Welcome back, Lord de Vere, we have quite forgot the fart.'

QUEEN ELIZABETH II (b. 1926)

Discussing the song 'Old MacDonald had a farm':

I know the song and I can make all the noises at home but I cannot do them with a tiara on.

When Fred Astaire reminded her once that he had danced with her mother:

You mean *she* danced with *you*.

QUEEN ELIZABETH THE QUEEN MOTHER (b. 1900; wife of King George VI)

Replying to a request from her daughter for a glass of wine:

My dear, do you think you should? After all, you have to reign all afternoon.

When the television was switched on for a football match and the crowd could be heard singing the National Anthem:

Oh, do turn it off. It is so embarrassing unless one is there – like hearing the Lord's Prayer when playing canasta.

MRS ALICE KEPPEL (1869–1947; mistress of King Edward VII)
A royal mistress should curtsy first – and then jump into bed.

BETTE MIDLER (b. 1945; American actress, comedienne and singer)
On Princess Anne:
Such an active lass. So outdoorsy. She loves nature in spite of what it did to her.

MRS PAUL PHIPPS (mother of English actress Joyce Grenfell)
When royalty leaves the room it is like getting a seed out of your tooth.

JOAN RIVERS (b. 1939; American comedienne)
Prince Charles's ears are so big he could hang-glide over the Falklands.

STEVIE SMITH (1902–71; English poet)
Describing her investiture by the Queen:
[It] was rather like meeting the very best sort of headmistress in the very best sort of mood.

ELIZABETH TAYLOR (b. 1932; English film actress)
At a film première Princess Margaret took note of the huge diamond on Miss Taylor's finger and said casually, 'That's a bit vulgar.'
   Unperturbed, Miss Taylor persuaded the Princess to try on the ring and when it was safely displayed on the Royal finger quipped, 'There, it's not so vulgar now, is it?'

SEX

TALLULAH BANKHEAD (1902–68; American actress, also known for her outrageous lifestyle)
Her ex-lover Lord Alington was dining with one of his parents and looked the other way so as not to see her enter the restaurant

with a friend: 'Darling,' she cried, 'don't you recognize me with my clothes on?

MRS PATRICK CAMPBELL (1865–1940; English actress)
To vegetarian George Bernard Shaw:
Shaw, someday you'll eat a beef steak and then no woman in London will be safe.

On being told of a homosexual affair between two actors:
I don't care what people do, as long as they don't do it in the street and frighten the horses!

JILLY COOPER (b. 1937; English writer and humorist)
Most of the upper classes share beds with their dogs for warmth. When a lover leaps into bed and thinks he has encountered something interesting and furry, he may easily get bitten!

From *Class*:
The best lover of all is the upper-middle-class intellectual. Having been made to run round by his mother when he was young he's into role reversal and a woman having as much pleasure as a man. Lucky the girl that lays the golden egghead.

From *Super-Jilly*:
Sex is only the liquid centre of the great Newberry Fruit of friendship.

PHYLLIS DILLER (b. 1917; American comedienne)
Nothing was happening in my marriage. I nicknamed our waterbed Lake Placid.

EDNA FERBER (1887–1967; American writer)
A woman can look both moral and exciting – if she also looks as if it was quite a struggle.

ZSA ZSA GABOR (b. ?1918; Hungarian-born actress; Miss Hungary 1936; seven times married)
I know nothing about sex, because I was always married.

ELINOR GLYN (1864–1943; English novelist and Hollywood script writer, famous for her erotic writing)

As lovers:

Americans	–	Fatherly and uncouth
French	–	Passionate and *petit maitre*
Austrian	–	Sentimental and feckless
Hungarian	–	Passionate and exacting
Scandinavian	–	Psychological and scientific
Russian	–	Passionate and unstable
Spanish	–	Jealous and matter of fact
Italian	–	Romantic and fickle
English	–	Casual and adorable
German	–	Sentimental and vulgar
All the near East	–	Passionate and untrustworthy

GERMAINE GREER (b. 1939; Australian writer)

Conventional heterosexual intercourse is like squirting jam into a doughnut.

SARAH HARRISON (b. 1946; English writer)

Faint heart never won fair lay.

JOYCE JILLSON (contemporary American writer)

From *Real Women Don't Pump Gas*:

Q.: What is a Real Woman's idea of succesful foreplay?

A.: Flowers, dinner, and a movie.

The only place a Real Woman can't really enjoy sex is in her parents' house – after she's married. This is ironic because, before she got married, it was the only place she *could*.

CHRISTINE KEELER (b. 1942; English former call-girl at the centre of the Profumo scandal)

Sex to Peter Rachman was like cleaning his teeth, and I was the toothpaste.

MRS ALFRED KINSEY (wife of the American sexologist working in the 1940s and 1950s)

I don't see so much of Alfred any more since he got so interested in sex.

EVELYN LAYE (b. 1900; English actress and singer)

Sex, unlike justice, should not be seen to be done.

MAUREEN LIPMAN (b. 1946; English actress and writer)

You know the worst thing about oral sex? The view.

ALICE ROOSEVELT LONGWORTH (1884–1980; American, daughter of President Theodore Roosevelt; nicknamed 'Princess Malice')

On her one pregnancy, at the age of forty-two, after eighteen years of marriage:

I'm always willing to try anything once.

On her ninetieth birthday, talking about life and love in the days of her youth:

In those days people were always having love affairs with their poodles and putting tiny flowers in strange places.

LYDIA LOPOKOVA (1892–1981; Russian, Diaghilev ballet dancer and wife of economist John Maynard Keynes)

On lesbianism, in conversation with a friend:

Two men – yes – I can see they've got something to take hold of. But two women – that's impossible. You can't have two insides having an affair!

MARYA MANNES (b. 1904; American jouranlist and essayist)

Flirtation is merely an expression of considered desire coupled with an admission of its impracticability.

PRINCESS METTERNICH (1836–1921; Austrian)

When asked, 'When does a woman cease being capable of sexual love?':

You must ask someone else. I am only sixty.

BETTE MIDLER (b. 1945; American actress, comedienne and singer)

I married a German – every night I dress up as Poland and he invades me.

MISTINGUETT (stage name of Jeanne Bourgeois; ?1874–1956; French singer and dancer)

A kiss can be a comma, a question mark or an exclamation point. That's basic spelling that every woman ought to know.

DOROTHY PARKER (1893–1967; American writer, satirist and humorist)

'General Review of the Sex Situation':

Woman wants monogamy;
Man delights in novelty.
Love is woman's moon and sun;
Man has other forms of fun.
Woman lives but in her lord;
Count to ten, and man is bored.
With this the gist and sum of it,
What earthly good can come of it?

JOAN RIVERS (b. 1939; American comedienne)

The only time a woman has a true orgasm is when she's shopping. Every other time she's faking it. It's common courtesy.

From *The Life and Hard Times of Heidi Abromowitz*:

[Heidi] told me that lately when she passed a motel, she had a feeling of déjà screw.

ADELA ROGERS ST JOHNS (b. 1894; American journalist and writer)

Mrs [Margaret] Sanger said the best birth control is to make your husband sleep on the roof.

SALLY STANFORD (1904–82; American civic leader and writer)

No man can be held throughout the day by what happens through the night.

MAE WEST (1892–1980; American, 'world's greatest movie siren')

Too much of a good thing can be wonderful.

When I'm good, I'm very good, but when I'm bad, I'm better.

Don't crowd me, boys – there's enough for everybody.

Let's face it, the sex organs ain't got no personality.

On being told a new male acquaintance was 6'7'':

Let's forget about the six feet and talk about the seven inches.

On her love affair with George Raft:

It was love on the run with half the buttons undone. The results were like a high-speed film – blurred but excitin'.

To Raquel Welch:

Honey, I used to have censor trouble when a man even sat on my lap. Since then I've had more men on my lap than table napkins.

MARY DAY WINN (1888–1965; American writer)

Sex is the tabasco sauce which an adolescent national palate sprinkles on every course in the menu.

SNOBBERY

NANCY ASTOR (1879–1964; American-born British politician. First woman to take her seat in the House of Commons)

To console Grace Vanderbilt for being placed behind Nancy in precedence at a dinner given by the Theodore Roosevelts:

The Astors skinned skunks a hundred years before the Vanderbilts worked ferries.

JANE AUSTEN (1775–1817; English novelist)
From *Persuasion*:

If he should ever be made a Baronet! 'Lady Wentworth' sounds very well. That would be a noble thing, indeed, for Henrietta! She would take place of me then, and Henrietta would not dislike that. Sir Frederick and Lady Wentworth! It would be but a new creation, however, and I never think much of your new creations.

LADY AYLESBURY (fl. 1600–50, wife of Sir Thomas Aylesbury)
[Attributed]

Always be nice to girls, you never know who they will marry.

MARGARET AYER BARNES (1886–1967; American writer)
From *Years of Grace*:

'Curious, isn't it,' he went on airily, 'that "talking with the right people" means something so very different from "talking with the right person"?'

MIRIAM BEARD (b. 1901; American feminist writer and humorist)
Describing a shopping expedition in New York to buy a gift for a friend:

'Haven't you some small article I could send her, very attractive – typically American?'

The sales expert in the shop looked depressed . . . 'American, you say? . . . Why, my dee-ur, *we* don't carry those *Colonial* goods. All *our* things are *imported*.'

BARBARA CARTLAND (b. 1902; English romantic novelist)

One of the rudest things is a man walking around with his hands in his pockets. James Laver said that whenever women dropped their necklines and took off their corsets you got high inflation and bad manners. Well, there you are.

Miss Cartland has always staunchly upheld the traditional values and a true fairytale romance came into her life when her own daughter's step-daughter, Lady Diana Spencer, married the Prince of Wales in 1981. As a result Miss Cartland was interviewed many times on television and radio and on one occasion was asked whether she thought class barriers had become less important in Britain. 'Of course they have,' she replied, 'otherwise I wouldn't be here talking to someone like you!'

COLETTE (1873–1954; French novelist)

From *Gigi*:

'Call your mother, Gigi! Liane d'Exelmans has committed suicide.'

The child replied with a long drawn out, 'Ooh!' and asked 'Is she dead?'

'Of course not. She knows how to do things properly.'

JILLY COOPER (b. 1937; English writer and humorist)

With the inroads of women's lib, upper middle-class women are less and less often shunted off to drink coffee by themselves after dinner, the merry-tocracy in particular believing in a port in every girl.

From *Class*:

'Are you a titled Mummy's nanny?' said one gorgon, when a newly employed nanny sat down beside her.

The new nanny shook her head.

'Well I'm afraid,' said the gorgon, 'that this bench is reserved for titled mummies' nannies.'

LILLIAN DAY (20th c. American writer)

A lady is one who never shows her underwear unintentionally.

GEORGE ELIOT (1819–80; English novelist)

Correct English is the slang of prigs.

FASCINATING AIDA (trio of British female singers/comediennes, 1980s)

Extract from one of their songs:

We can say with clarity
We *don't* believe in social parity
For if everyone were equal
We couldn't work for charity.

ISABELLA STEWART (Mrs Jack) GARDNER (1840–1924; American socialite)

Born in New York, Isabella Gardner had great difficulty being accepted by the most élite and snobbish elements of Boston society. One day one of the worst of these women condescended to call on her in order to collect a donation to Boston's charitable Eye and Ear Association.

'Gracious,' replied 'Mrs Jack, 'I didn't think there was a single charitable eye or ear in the whole of Boston.'

Bored by Boston people boasting about their ancestors coming over on the *Mayflower*, Mrs Jack remarked: 'Indeed, I understand the immigration laws are much stricter nowadays.'

JOYCE GRENFELL (1910–79; English comedienne and writer)

From *Nanny Says*:

We don't like that girl from Tooting Bec,
She washes her face and forgets her neck.

MRS HARRINGTON GREY (late 19th-early 20th c. American socialite)

Asked whether or not her family had arrived from England on the first or second boat, Boston socialite Mrs Harrington Grey neatly avoided potential social ignominy by replying: 'We sent our servants ahead on the first boat to get things ready for us.'

ROSA LEWIS (1867–1952; English hotelier and former mistress of King Edward VII)

Lowly-born Rosa Lewis had been one of Edward VII's mistresses. Later she became the proprietor of the Cavendish Hotel, which was famous for its good food and as a favourite place for 'assignations'. When Mrs Patrick Campbell, the actress, was seriously ill Rosa Lewis visited her frequently with delicious delicacies from her own kitchens, but she was pointedly ignored by some of Mrs Campbell's aristocratic visitors. She related one such incident to the patient without any sense of mortification but rather with satisfaction, remarking of their respective furs: 'Me in my sinful sables and 'er in 'er virtuous cat!'

MARIE LLOYD (1870–1922; English cockney music hall star)

Although she was infinitely the most popular and charismatic of variety performers of her day Marie Lloyd was deliberately omitted from the 1911 Royal Command Performance as a calculated snub because of her recent divorce. Refusing to be crushed, Miss Lloyd appeared the same evening at a theatre a few yards away, her posters carrying the message, 'Every performance given by Marie Lloyd is a Command Performance by order of the British public.'

LADY VERONICA MCLEOD (fl. 1890s)

Quoted in *Great Sexual Disasters*:

The late Lady Veronica McLeod had style. She was the only daughter of a distinguished British General and in the London of the 1890s she was a celebrated beauty. It was then the heyday of the British Raj and her father had been stationed in India for some years. When she was nineteen she sailed out to visit him and on the crossing fell head over heels in love with a handsome young steward in second class. At the ship's fancy dress ball they managed to dance together all evening and then slipped away to Veronica's cabin where they spent a blissful night. The following morning the young steward had to be up long before his lady-love in order to serve breakfast to his passengers. When he caught up with Lady Veronica later in the day and began to talk to her she reproved him icily for his familiarity: 'In the circles in which I move, sleeping with a woman does not constitute an introduction.'

NANCY MITFORD (1904–73; English novelist and biographer)

From *The Pursuit of Love*:

Uncle Matthew: Education! I was always led to suppose that no educated person ever spoke of notepaper, and yet I hear poor Fanny asking Sadie for notepaper. What is this education? Fanny talks about mirrors and mantelpieces, handbags and perfume, she takes sugar in her coffee, has a tassel on her umbrella, and I have no doubt that if she is ever fortunate enough to catch a husband she will call his father and mother Father and Mother. Will the wonderful education she is getting make up to the unhappy brute for all these endless pinpricks? Fancy hearing one's wife talk about notepaper – the irritation!

HANNAH MORE (1745–1833; English writer and moralist)

In men this blunder still you find –
All think their little set mankind.

ANNE OLIVER (contemporary American director of L'Ecole des Ingenues of Atlanta, Paris, London and Aspen)

I always say being finished is knowing your Manet from your Monet.

LADY VICTOR PAGET (English friend of King Edward VIII)

How vulgar of these American women to call him David. Either one calls him Sir or one calls him Darling.

DOROTHY PARKER (1893–1967; American writer, satirist and humorist)

Dorothy Parker and Elsa Maxwell were lunching with a particularly obnoxious man who was determined to make Elsa feel intellectually inferior. The conversation turned to art, and the man, after making it clear that he was an intimate friend of the painter Augustus John, turned patronisingly to Miss Maxwell and said, 'Of course, I don't suppose you know who I'm talking about.'

'Oh yes she does,' countered Dorothy Parker. 'But they're such great friends she calls him Augustus Jack.'

MARY PETTIBONE POOLE (American writer)

Culture is what your butcher would have if he were a surgeon.

MRS BARCLAY SCULL (19th c. American socialite)

Most of the Biddles and Cadwaladers [Philadelphian families of distinction] are now either in front of bars or behind bars.

DAME EDITH SITWELL (1887–1966; eccentric English poet)

To an American newspaper man who demanded to know why she called herself 'Dame':

I don't. The Queen does.

MURIEL SPARK (b. 1918; English writer)

From *The Prime of Miss Jean Brodie*:

'Whoever has opened the window has opened it too wide,' said Miss Brodie. 'Six inches is perfectly adequate. More is vulgar.'

COUNTESS SPENCER (b. 1929; step-mother of the Princess of Wales)

Nothing is more debasing for a real man than a plastic apron.

LADY WILSON (19th c.; Scottish-born writer who lived for 20 years in India)

From *Letters From India*:

'The tale goes that an irate Colonel, who had just heard where his place was to be at the dinner table, said to his charming hostess that, "Of course it was a matter of no importance, but he thought in his position he ought to tell her he was a full Colonel." She only said, "Are you really? Well I hope that when dinner is over you will be still fuller!"'

VIRGINIA WOOLF (1882–1941; English novelist)

Those comfortably padded lunatic asylums which are known, euphemistically, as the stately homes of England.

SUCCESS

DAME LILIAN BRAITHWAITE (1873–1948; English actress)

From *Distinguished Company*, by John Gielgud:

Her kindness was unfailing, but the subtely of the pause she would give to cap a critical remark could be delightfully pungent and occasionally devastating. 'B. told me that she is off to do a play in New York tomorrow . . . but I don't think it can be a very big part as she is going on a very small boat.'

CORAL BROWNE (b. 1913; Australian-born actress)

Jill Bennett and Coral Browne were cast together in a play which was due to make a lengthy tour before eventually coming to London. At the first reading both actresses took stock of the young male actors in the company and discovered that the majority of them appeared to be homosexual. However, there was one who seemed to be both beefy and butch and they mutually decided that this was the only one they both found attractive. Coral was inclined to believe that there was some chance of success with the young man but Jill Bennett was less optimistic.

'Well, darling,' said Coral, 'we have got six weeks in darkest Newcastle, Birmingham and Manchester, and a lot can happen by then.'

'In that case,' her friend replied, 'you're on your own. Although he's attractive I don't intend to waste my time, but I'm willing to bet *you* a pound that you won't get him in to bed before we reach London.'

The weeks passed and in Brighton, the last week before the tour ended, Jill Bennett was convinced that Coral Browne had lost her pound. However, Miss Browne refused to admit defeat – there were still another seven days to go.

When the tour ended the cast met up at the Queen's Theatre in preparation for the London first night and, following theatrical tradition, Coral, the leading lady, was the last to arrive. As she passed the seated Jill Bennett to take her place, she said in a loud whispered aside, 'Oh, by the way, Jill – I owe you 7/6d.'

DAME GLADYS COOPER (1888–1971; English actress)

When her grandson Wilton wrote to her that at school he'd been told she had been the Marilyn Monroe of her day, she wrote back: 'I suppose it was true that I was the pin-up girl of my time and she of hers but I was pinned up for quite *different* reasons.'

DAME EDITH EVANS (1888–1973; English actress)

God was very good to me. He never let me go on tour.

JEAN GRAMAN

If at first you don't succeed, you're fired!

HEDY LAMARR (b. 1914; Austrian-born film star)

Any girl can be glamorous; all you have to do is stand still and look stupid.

FRAN LEBOWITZ (b. 1951; American writer)

From *Metropolitan Life*:

12.35 p.m. The phone rings. I am not amused. This is not my favourite way to wake up. My favourite way to wake up is to have a certain French movie star whisper to me softly at 2.30 in the afternoon that if I want to get to Sweden in time to pick up my Nobel Prize for Literature I had better ring for breakfast. This occurs rather less often than one might wish.

MAUREEN LIPMAN (b. 1946; English actress and writer)

The standards women set for themselves these days are incredibly high and we can't live up to them. Whatever we do, we can never make the perfect soufflé – and be up in the bedroom in the black lacy underwear at the right time, or, if we are, the plumber's bound to be in there.

MARY WILSON LITTLE (19th c.; American writer)

The penalty of success is to be bored by the attentions of people who formerly snubbed you.

MARQUISE DE MAINTENON (1635–1719; French mistress of King Louis XIV)

As Madame de Montespan, one of Louis XIV's earlier mistresses, passed her on the stairs, she observed, 'You are going down, Madame, I am going up.'

MARILYN MONROE (1926–62; American actress)

I've been on a calendar, but never on *Time*.

ELIZABETH MONTAGU (1720–1800; English writer and prominent 'Blue-Stocking')

Asked the secret of her successful parties she sensibly replied, 'No idiots were ever invited.'

MARYON PEARSON (1897–1972; wife of Canadian Prime Minister Lester Pearson)

Behind every successful man stands a surprised woman.

JOAN RIVERS (b. 1939; American comedienne)

All a woman needs is a pretty face and a trick pelvis and she's home and dry.

ADELA ROGERS ST JOHNS (b. 1894; American journalist and writer)

I've often thought that if Nixon had made the football team, his life would have been different.

ELIZABETH TAYLOR (b. 1932; English film actress)

If someone was stupid enough to offer me a million dollars to make a picture, I was certainly not dumb enough to turn it down.

RAQUEL WELCH (b. 1940; American actress)

I can't say the mini made me an actress but it sure helped make me a star.

MAE WEST (1892–1980; American, 'world's greatest movie siren')

It's not what I do but how I do it. It ain't what I say, but how I say it, and how I look when I do it and say it.

On her Broadway play *Sex* turning from flop to overnight success, she said it was a result of 'Mouth-to-mouth advertising – which is the best kind.'

It don't mean a thing if you don't pull a string.

CHARLOTTE WHITTON (1896–1975; Canadian writer and politician)

Whatever women do they must do twice as well as men to be thought half as good. Luckily, this is not difficult.

TRAVEL

ADELINE AINSWORTH

A trip is what you take when you can't take any more of what you've been taking.

ELENA PETROVNA BLAVATSKY (1831–91; Russian writer)

Just back from under the far-reaching shadow of the Eighth Wonder of the World – the gigantic iron carrot that goes by the name of the Eiffel Tower.

QUEEN ELIZABETH THE QUEEN MOTHER (b. 1900; wife of King George VI)

On the reason for the helicopter being her favourite means of transport:

The chopper has changed my life as conclusively as that of Ann Boleyn.

EVA JAGGER (mother of rock star, Mick Jagger)

The women in my family went to Australia to get away from the men.

MARY KINGSLEY (1862–1900; English explorer)

From *Travels in West Africa*:

Having been knocked to the bottom of the boat during a nerve-wracking sea journey:

There is nothing like entering into the spirit of a thing like this if you mean to enjoy it, . . . for there's nothing between enjoying it and dying of it!

From *Travels in West Africa*:

All West African steamers have a mania for bush, and the delusion that they are required to climb trees. The *Fallabar* had the complaint severely, because of her defective steering powers, and the temptation the magnificent forest, and the rapid currents, and the sharp turns of the creek district, offered her; she failed, of course – they all fail – but it is not for want of practice. I have seen many West Coast vessels up trees, but never more than fifteen feet or so.

From *Travels in West Africa*:

Meeting the Chief of Police at Libreville, French West Africa: The chief is clad in a white shirt and white pantaloons cut *à la* Turque, but unfortunately these garments have a band that consists of a run-in string, and that string is out of repair. He writes furiously – blotting paper mislaid – frantic flurry round – pantaloons won't stand it – grab just saves them – something wanted the other side of the room – headlong flight towards it – 'now's our chance,' think the pantaloons, and make off – recaptured.

Formalities being concluded regarding us, the chief makes a dash out from behind his writing-table, claps his heels together, and bows with a jerk that causes the pantaloons to faint in coils, like the White Knight in 'Alice in Wonderland' . . .

PRINCESS MARGARET (b. 1930)
Going to Morocco is rather like being kidnapped – you never know where you are going or with whom!

BETTE MIDLER (b. 1945; American actress, comedienne and singer)
I knew so little of the world, really. Slander, not geography, had always been my strongest suit.

146

DERVLA MURPHY (b. 1931; Irish travel writer)

From *Full Tilt*:

Tehran, 30 March: – I've always been advised that hotel bedrooms without locks call for empty bottles balanced on top of the door to ensure that one is not taken altogether by surprise should wandering lechers have designs on one's virtue. (As creating empty bottles is one of the few things I'm good at, this is an appropriate suggestion.)

JOAN RIVERS (b. 1939; American comedienne)

Omaha is a little like Newark – without Newark's glamour.

IRENE THOMAS (b. 1920; English writer and broadcaster)

From *The Bandsman's Daughter*:

The Thai people were the most elegant I've ever seen – all of them, men and women, tiny and exquisite, as though God had made them to put on his mantlepiece.

UNDERSTATEMENT

NANCY ASTOR (1879–1964; American-born British politician. First woman to take her seat in the House of Commons)

Replying to a question about police arresting young women in the streets:

I must tell you something awfully funny that happened to me in London the other day. I saw a young American sailor outside the House of Commons. I said to him, 'Would you like to go in?' and he said, 'You're the sort of woman my mother warned me against.' I went to Admiral Sims that night, and said to him, 'Admiral, you have one perfectly upright young man in the American Navy.'

TALLULAH BANKHEAD (1902–68; American actress, known for her outrageous lifestyle as much as her acting)

I'm pure as the driven slush.

When I heard that Bette Davis was playing me in *All About Eve* I said, 'Hasn't she always?'

DJUNA BARNES (1892–1982; American writer)
From 'What Do You See, Madam?'

'Billy,' she said, and her voice was cold and practical, 'I couldn't ever boil potatoes over the heat of your affection.'

DAME LILIAN BRAITHWAITE (1873–1948; English actress noted for her comedy roles)

Joyce Carey, Dame Lilian's actress daughter, tells the following story of an incident which occurred during the height of the London Blitz:

She and her mother were living in a flat in Chelsea but despite the bombing Dame Lilian refused to leave her flat for the shelter and Joyce Carey naturally felt she must stay with her mother. So it was that they were both asleep in their respective bedrooms when the infamous land mine which killed 75 people exploded. There was at least ten minutes of the most terrible noise, chaos and confusion, and when the hubbub began to die down Joyce found that her bed was buried almost a foot deep in plaster and rubble. Hardly able to move, and terrified of what she might find in the adjacent bedroom, she lay petrified. For about two minutes there was total and utter silence, and then through the partition wall she heard the stentorian tones of the great actress utter just two words: 'WELL!!! REALLY!!!'

CORAL BROWNE (b. 1913; Australian-born actress)
On seeing the 19-foot golden phallus which was the focal point of design for the play *Oedipus Rex*:

No one I know, darling.

When discussing the passionate but incongruous *affaire* between a distinguished elderly classical actor and a very young actress of her acquaintance:

I never knew what he saw in her until the day I saw her eating corn on the cob at the Caprice.

Coral Browne was appearing in a play in the Haymarket Theatre. One afternoon after rehearsal, when it was absolutely pouring with rain, she emerged from the theatre and hailed the only available taxi. At precisely the same moment a bowler-hatted, highly respectable young man hailed the same taxi from the other side of the road, without having caught sight of Miss Browne. As it stopped in the middle of the road he walked over and was about to open the door, saying to the driver, 'Mansion House, please,' when the driver said, 'Sorry, sir, but I saw the lady first.' Bemused, the man looked around the deserted, rain-swept street and said politely, 'What lady?' From the depths of the taxi, where she sat swathed in mink and sable, came the beautifully modulated tones of Miss Browne, who tapped her chest and growled at him: 'This fucking lady!'

DAME GLADYS COOPER (1888–1971; English actress)

Looking into her mirror, the day before she died:

If this is what virus pneumonia does to one, I really don't think I shall bother to have it again.

QUEEN ELIZABETH II (b. 1926)

Commenting on Niagara Falls:

It looks very damp.

At a reception in Lisbon, 1957, to a BBC engineer 'caught out' on her arrival:

Good evening, Mr Jackson, shouldn't you be shining that light on me?

JUDY GARLAND (1922–69; American singer and actress)

Asked on a television chat show whether or not she agreed that a famous Hollywood star was a nymphomaniac she agreed – 'But only if you calm her down.'

PRINCESS GRACE OF MONACO (1928–82; American film actress who married Prince Rainier III)

On an enormous emerald and ruby ring she always wore:

I like to know which is my starboard and port side.

LUCILLE S. HARPER
Quoted in *Quotations For Our Time*:

One nice thing about egotists: they don't talk about other people.

JEAN KERR (b. 1923; American playwright and essayist)

If you can keep your head when all about you are losing theirs, it's just possible you haven't grasped the situation.

MARIE LLOYD (1870–1922; English cockney music-hall star)

Miss Lloyd had been arrested and subjected to several hours of close questioning because she arrived in America in the company of a man who was not her husband. When she finally emerged an ingenuous reporter asked, 'What is your opinion of America, Miss Lloyd?' Wryly she indicated the nearby Statue of Liberty and answered, 'See that? Well, I think that your idea of humour is – grand.'

PRINCESS LOUISE (1848–1939; daughter of Queen Victoria)

Princess Louise was the most spirited of Queen Victoria's daughters and least inclined to succumb to the restrictions of her position. Some years after the Queen's death she and several of her brothers and sisters were at a memorial service in the Queen's mausoleum. As they prayed a dove came into the building and flew above their heads. Delighted by the symbolism they all agreed it was 'dear Mama's spirit', except Louise.

'But of course it is,' the others insisted.

'It certainly is not,' said Princess Louise firmly, 'Dear Mama's spirit would never have ruined Beatrice's hat.'

QUEEN MARY (1867–1953; consort of King George V)
When her husband first went down in a submarine:

I shall be very disappointed if George doesn't come up again.

AGNES SMEDLEY (b. ?1894–1950; American lecturer and writer)
There's something dreadfully decisive about a beheading.

GERTRUDE STEIN (1874–1946; American writer)
Honesty is a selfish virtue. Yes, I am honest enough.

CAROL TAVRIS (contemporary American feminist writer)
Quoted in *Picking on Men*:
The daughter of a friend took her first bath with a male cousin
when they were both four years old. Being well brought up, she
was silent about her anatomical discovery, but that night, as her
mother tucked her into bed, she said, 'Mommy, isn't it a blessing
he doesn't have it on his face?'
    So much for penis envy.

KIRI TE KANAWA (b. 1944; New Zealand opera singer)
I'm anorexic for an opera singer . . . but I'm a fat anorexic.

QUEEN VICTORIA (1819–1901)
On being told by an East End clergyman that in one house he
visited seven people slept in one bed:
Had I been one of them I would have slept on the floor.

MAE WEST (1892–1980; American, 'world's greatest movie
siren')
I used to be Snow White, but I drifted.

VANITY – AND LACK OF IT

NANCY ASTOR (1879–1964; American-born British politician.
First woman to take her seat in the House of Commons)
I am the kind of woman I would run away from.

To Winston Churchill, who said a woman's presence in the

House of Commons was as embarrassing as if she had entered his bathroom when he only had a sponge with which to defend himself:

You are not handsome enough to have worries of that kind.

TALLULAH BANKHEAD (1902–68; American actress, also known for her outrageous lifestlye)

They used to photograph Shirley Temple through gauze. They should photograph me through linoleum.

ELEANOR BRON (b. 1934; English actress)

Included in her list of Pathetic Things (from *The Pillow Book of Eleanor Bron*):

A woman who has taken just too long to understand that she is physically attractive, perhaps even beautiful; her beautiful sisters have had a lifetime to fritter away their inheritance; she has lost a legacy just the day after hearing the Will read.

MRS PATRICK CAMPBELL (1865–1940; English actress)

I look like a burst paper bag . . . I must borrow a chair with a high back so that I can hide my chins behind it.

My eyes are really nothing in particular . . . God gave me boot buttons, but I invented the dreamy eyelid, and that makes all the difference.

COCO CHANEL (1883–1971; French *couturière*)

Hell hath no vanity like a handsome man.

COLETTE (1873–1954; French novelist)

From *Chéri*:

Give me a dozen such heartbreaks if that would help me lose a couple of pounds.

PHYLLIS DILLER (b. 1917; American comedienne)

If my jeans could talk they'd plead for mercy.

MARY DUNN (1900–58; English writer and social satirist, best known for her 'Lady Addle' books)

A cure for bags under the eyes (from *The World of Lady Addle*):

Sleep upside down and the bags will often work through to a less noticeable part of the body.

GEORGE ELIOT (1819–80; English novelist)

From *The Mill on the Floss*:

I've never any pity for conceited people, because I think they carry their comfort about with them.

LADY CARINA FROST (b. 1952; daughter of Britain's leading Roman Catholic layman, the Duke of Norfolk)

Shortly before her marriage to television personality David Frost, Lady Carina was asked whether her intended husband was at all religious: 'Oh, yes,' she affirmed, 'he thinks he is God.'

LILLIAN HELLMAN (1905–84; American playwright and writer)

On movie tycoon Sam Goldwyn:

To understand Sam you must realise that he regards himself as a nation.

ELSA LANCHESTER (b. 1902; English-born actress)

After receiving a few lessons of Hindu dancing and belly dancing:

I only wanted to learn a smattering of other dance systems. I realized a smattering was enough to be an authority, which was all I wanted to be.

MARIE LLOYD (1870–1922; English cockney music-hall star)

One of her 'theme' songs:

I'm one of the ruins that Cromwell knocked about a bit.

DAME NELLIE MELBA (1861–1931; Australian opera singer)

After appearing at a musical soirée:

What a dreadful concert this would have been if I hadn't come.

MARILYN MONROE (1926–62; American actress)

We were asked to stick our footprints in wet concrete in front of Grauman's Chinese Theatre, along with the dent left by Jimmy Durante's nose and the print of one of Betty Grable's legs. I suggested that Jane [Russell] lean over the wet cement so her front would poke holes in it, and that I sit down in it, and we could leave our most important measurements that way, but my idea was vetoed.

MARGARET OLIPHANT (1828–97; English writer)

From *Salem Chapel*:

'I am perfectly safe – nobody can possibly be safer than such a woman as I am, in poverty and middle age,' said this strange acquaintance. 'It is an immunity that women don't often prize, Mr Vincent, but it is very valuable in its way.'

MADAME DE POMPADOUR (1721–64; mistress of Louis XV of France)

On the fall of Quebec:

It makes little difference; Canada is useful only to provide me with furs.

JOAN RIVERS (b. 1939; American comedienne)

My thighs are so wobbly thank God my stomach covers them. I woke up this morning – I saw liver spots on my hands – I thought, Oh God, my nipples have moved.

My body is so bad a Peeping Tom looked in my window and pulled down the shade.

I gave my husband his heart attack. We were making love and I took the paper bag off my head.

I've got no bosoms, in Africa they want to name an underdeveloped nation after me.

I have no sex appeal – I have to blindfold my vibrator.

GEORGE SAND (1804–76; French writer)

From 'Horace':

She prided herself on being educated, erudite and eccentric. She had read a little of everything, even of politics and philosophy, and it was curious to hear her bringing out as her own, for the delectation of the ignorant, things that she had read that same morning in a book, or had heard the night before from the lips of some serious-minded man of her acquaintance.

DAME EDITH SITWELL (1887–1966; eccentric English poet)

I have often wished I had time to cultivate modesty – but I am too busy thinking about myself.

DAME SYBIL THORNDIKE (1882–1976; English actress)

Dame Sybil was one of the most distinguished actresses on the British stage. On one occasion she was appearing with the equally senior and revered actress Dame Edith Evans. The theatre's manager was agonising about which of these should be allocated the number one dressing room and finally went to Dame Sybil to confess his problem. Carefully he explained that both rooms were equally large and comfortable, but the number two dressing room was up a steep flight of stairs.

'Well then there's no problem,' Dame Sybil reassured him. 'Dame Edith must have the number one dressing room – *I* can still climb stairs.'

CAROLYN WELLS (1869–1942; American humorist and writer)

Limerick:

For beauty I am not a star.
There are others more handsome by far;
    But my face I don't mind it,
    For I am behind it.
It's the people in front that I jar.

MAE WEST (1892–1980; American, 'world's greatest movie siren')

An actor's toupée slipped over one eye in an amorous scene:

Don't look now, honey,' she murmured, 'but your hair's skiddin'.

SHELLEY WINTERS (b. 1922; American actress)
Of her ex-husband Vittorio Gassman:

He used to grab me in his arms, hold me close – and tell me how wonderful he was.

WAR

CARYL BRAHMS (b. ?1900–82; English comic novelist and scriptwriter)
From *No Nightingales* (with S.J. Simon):

You're a pessimist. What are facts? We'd never win a war if we faced facts.

CORAL BROWNE (b. 1913; Australian-born actress)

On the first day of the Second World War the indecision and panic which affected everyone was understandably apparent in the theatrical world. At the first reading of a new play in which Coral Browne was to star young actresses were weeping and young actors were tense and anxious at the thought that they might soon be in uniform. Realising that nothing was to be gained by continuing with the reading the director suggested they adjourn until impresario Binkie Beaumont had had time to readjust his plans. One young actress turned her tear-stained face to Coral, who was currently living with Firth Sheppard, one of London's most powerful and successful theatrical producers, and sobbed, 'What do you think is going to happen to us all?' Unperturbed, Miss Browne replied calmly, and with great faith, 'Firth is my shepherd, I shall not want.'

PATRICIA COCKBURN (b. 1914; Irish travel writer)
On an incident during the Irish troubles, from *Figure of Eight*:

Very few of the Anglo-Irish got shot, though a great deal of property was destroyed. A minor contributory factor to this latter fact may have been the silly story that was going around at the time among the Anglo-Irish, in which the head gardener of a Great House was supposed to have written to the absentee owner saying, 'We had a battle here last week but fortunately no one was hurt, and both sides greatly admired the antirrhinums.'

QUEEN ELIZABETH I (1533–1603)

When warned of impending hostilities by King Philip of Spain:

I cannot find it in me to fear a man who took ten years a-learning his alphabet.

VIRGINIA GRAHAM (b. 1912; American writer)

From *A Lullaby in Poor Taste*:

Lully my darling, till atom bombs fall,
When up will go baby and mummy and all.

QUEEN MARY (1867–1953; Consort of King George V)

At an early stage during the War Queen Mary paid a visit to an evacuation station to bring a little comfort to some of the many children who had been bombed out of their homes and forced to take refuge in such shelters. Exchanging pleasantries with a nine-year-old urchin, she enquired, 'And where do you live?'

'Back'a Selfridges,' he replied. 'Where d'you?'

Immediately Her Majesty, whose home was Marlborough House, answered, 'Back'a Fortnums.'

NANCY MITFORD (1904–73; British novelist and biographer)

Itemising the horrors of wartime:

The last straw is that Harrods don't stamp one's notepaper any more.

BARBRA STREISAND (b. 1942; Jewish-American singer and film actress)

On the furore among the Jewish/Arab communities for casting her with Egyptian-born Omar Sharif in *Funny Girl* during the Six Day War:

You think Cairo was upset – you should see the letter I got from my Aunt Rose.

DAME REBECCA WEST (1892–1983; English novelist and critic)

After the Second World War a Nazi death list was made public which included Dame Rebecca and her old friend Noel Coward. Dame Rebecca promptly cabled to Coward: 'My Dear, the people we should have been seen dead with.'

WOMEN

LUCILLE BALL (b. 1911; American comedy actress)

I believe a woman's place is in the home – or anyway in some cosy nightclub.

MARIA BASHKIRTSEFF (1860–84; Russian diarist and painter)

In my opinion, to a woman who knows her own mind men can only be a minor consideration.

HELEN BOEHM (b. ?1925; American businesswoman and socialite)

On the jet-set life of Palm Beach, Florida:

Once you've met the women, you can see why the men have died or run away.

CARYL BRAHMS (b. ?1900–82; English comic novelist and scriptwriter)

From *No Nightingales* (with S.J. Simon):

The suffragettes were triumphant. Woman's place was in the gaol.

MRS PATRICK CAMPBELL (1865–1940; English actress)

To the man sitting next to her at a New York dinner:

Do you know why God witheld the sense of humour from women? So that we may love you instead of laughing at you!

ELLEN COHN (American columnist)

Quoted in *Words and Women* by Casey Miller and Kate Swift:

Question: Who is credited with discovering radium?

Answer (all together): Madame Curie.

Well, class, the woman (who was indeed married to a man named Pierre Curie) had a first name all of her own. From now on let's call her Marie Curie.

Question: Can Madame Curie ever be appropriately used?

Answer: Of course. Whenever the inventor of the telephone is called Mr Bell.

GEORGE ELIOT (1819–80; English novelist)

From *Adam Bede*:

I'm not denyin' the women are foolish: God Almighty made 'em to match the men.

JOYCE GRENFELL (1910–79; English comedienne and writer)

From 'Stately as a Galleon':

Stately as a galleon, I sail across the floor,
Doing the Military Two-step, as in the days of yore.
I dance with Mrs Tiverton; she's light on her feet, in spite
Of turning the scale at fourteen stone, and being of medium
height.
So gay the band,
So giddy the sight,
Full evening dress is a must,
But the zest goes out of a beautiful waltz
When you dance it bust to bust.

EMMA LEE (American writer)

Not all women give most of their waking thoughts to the problem of pleasing men. Some are married.

CAROLE LOMBARD (1908–42; American film actress)

I live by a man's code, designed to fit a man's world, yet at the same time I never forget that a woman's first job is to choose the right shade of lipstick.

CLARE BOOTH LUCE (b. 1903; American writer, politician and diplomat)

If God had wanted us to think with our wombs why did he give us a brain?

ALICE DUER MILLER (1874–1942; American writer and poet)

From *Forsaking All Others*:

> When a woman like that whom I've seen too much
> All of a sudden drops out of touch,
> Is always busy and never can
> Spare you a moment, it means a Man.

LADY MARY WORTLEY MONTAGU (1689–1762; English letter-writer, notable for her *Letters from the East*, written while her husband was Ambassador at Constantinople in 1716; pioneer of smallpox vaccine)

It goes far towards reconciling me to being a woman when I reflect that I am thus in no danger of marrying one.

JILL RUCKELSHAUS (b. ?1937; American government official and lecturer)

It occurred to me when I was thirteen and wearing white gloves and Mary Janes and going to dancing school, that no one should have to dance backward all their lives.

ADELA ROGERS ST JOHNS (b. 1894; American journalist and writer)

God made man, and then said I can do better than that and made woman.

OLIVE SCHREINER (1855–1920; South African writer)

From *The Story of an African Farm*:

It is delightful to be a woman; but every man thanks the Lord devoutly that he isn't one.

CORNELIA OTIS SKINNER (1901–79; American actress and writer)

Woman's virtue is man's greatest invention.

SOPHIE TUCKER (?1884–1966; Jewish-American vaudeville and nightclub entertainer)

From birth to age eighteen, a girl needs good parents. From eighteen to thirty-five, she needs good looks. From thirty-five to fifty-five she needs a good personality. From fifty-five on, she needs good cash.

JILL TWEEDIE (b. 1936; English columnist and writer)

From *Letters from a Fainthearted Feminist*:

I'm so housebound these days I have to take Kwells to get to the greengrocers.

CAROLYN WELLS (1869–1942; American humorist and writer)

'The Spelling Lesson'

When Venus said 'Spell no for me,'
    'N-O,' Dan Cupid wrote with glee,
        And smiled at his success;
'Ah, child,' said Venus, laughing low,
'We women do not spell it so,
        'We spell it Y-E-S.'

'Woman'

But Woman is rare beyond compare,
The poets tell us so;
How little they know of Woman
Who only Women know!

KATHARINE WHITEHORN (contemporary English writer and broadcaster)

On gynaecology:

. . . the unkind folklore men cherish about the rest of women's cycles can make you despair; as if oest was oest and test was test and never the twain could meet.

XENOPHOBIA

MARGOT ASQUITH (1864–1945; English socialite and political hostess, wife of Prime Minister Herbert Asquith)

What a pity, when Christopher Columbus discovered America, that he ever mentioned it.

JANE AUSTEN (1775–1817; English novelist)

Mrs Elton in *Emma*:

One has no great hopes from Birmingham. I always say there is something direful in the sound.

CARYL BRAHMS (b. ?1900–82; English comic novelist and scriptwriter)

From *Don't Mr Disraeli* (with S.J. Simon):

Uncle Clarence had mistrusted Orientals ever since his ticket failed to win the Calcutta Sweep.

COLETTE (1873–1954; French novelist)

From *The Photographer's Missus*:

In our part of the world, as you well know, they say raw meat is for cats and the English.

VIRGINIE DEJAZET (1798–1875; French actress)

When her stolid companions at a dinner party in Berlin failed to muster a smile at any of her jokes she rounded on them, saying: 'My German friends, what you have been listening to is called wit. May I suggest you pool your resources in order to appreciate it.'

LADY DOCKER (1900–82; English socialite famous in the 1950s for her opulent lifestyle)

On Monaco, where she kept her yacht and which turned her out after she insulted the Monagasque flag at a party:

That little state like Hampstead Heath in the South of France.

FIONA FULLERTON (b. ?1956; English actress)

This man [in Los Angeles] said to me, 'Gee, you've got a great pair of tits. How much did they cost?'

HERMIONE GINGOLD (b. 1897; English actress)

I've discovered that what we in England call draughts you in America call cross-ventilation.

MARGARET HALSEY (b. 1910; American writer)

From *With Malice Toward Some*:

Whatever the rest of the world thinks of the English gentleman, the English lady regards him apprehensively as something between God and a goat, and equally formidable on both scores.

From *With Malice Toward Some*:

The English never smash in a face. They merely refrain from asking it to dinner.

LILLIAN HELLMAN (1905–84; American playwright and writer)

Years ago I heard somebody say that being a Roumanian was not a nationality but a profession.

FRAN LEBOWITZ (b. 1951; American writer)

On Paris (from *Metropolitan Life*):

If you're going there you would do well to remember this: no matter how politely or distinctly you ask a Parisian a question he will persist in answering you in French.

LYDIA LOPOKOVA (1892–1981; Russian, Diaghilev ballet dancer and wife of economist John Maynard Keynes)

So this is how we live in Russia, talking, drinking tea, supporting a hundred relations, though we do not find it necessary to write up what I find on the portal of every church in England *that a man may not marry his grandmother*.

DAME ROSE MACAULAY (1881–1958; English novelist and travel writer)

The great and recurrent question about abroad is – is it worth getting there?

DAME NELLIE MELBA (1861–1931; Australian opera singer)

Advice to Dame Clara Butt, prior to the latter's tour of Australia, c. 1907:

So you're going to Australia? Well, *I* made £20,000 on my tour there, but of course *that* won't be done again. Still, it's a wonderful country and you'll have a good time. What are you going to sing? All I can say is – sing 'em muck! It's all they can understand.

BETTE MIDLER (b. 1945; American actress, comedienne and singer)

On Australia:

Once you're out of Sydney, every town is Perth.

JESSICA MITFORD (b. 1917; English writer)

From *Hons and Rebels*:

Things on the whole are much faster in America; people don't *stand for election*, they *run for office*. If a person say he's *sick*, it doesn't mean regurgitating; it means *ill*. *Mad* means *angry*, not *insane*. Don't ask for the *left-luggage*; it's called a *check-room*. A *nice joint* means a *good pub*, not roast meat.

YOUTH

PRINCESS ANNE (b. 1950)

On being asked if she regretted not having a University education:

Oh no, I learnt all *that* in the Girl Guides.

LILIAN BAYLIS (1874–1937; English music-hall singer and founder of the Old Vic)

John Gielgud, who had enjoyed a successful season at the Old

Vic, was discussing future plans with Miss Baylis. Naively anxious to be taken seriously he told her that he would love to work with her again, but could not begin immediately because he had so many other engagements. Neatly turning the tables, Miss Baylis responded: 'That's right dear, you play all the young parts you can – while you're still able to.'

PHYLLIS DILLER (b. 1917; American singer and comedienne)

Miss Diller was explaining to a friend her theory that one invaluable method of holding the ageing process at bay was to take a succession of increasingly youthful lovers. When her friend asked her how to judge the age at which it would be prudent to draw the line, Miss Diller replied: 'If he starts sending you love letters written in crayon; if he can fly for half-fare; or if his pyjamas have feet.'

IDINA, COUNTESS OF ERROL (b. ?1903; English socialite)

Reresby Sitwell, nephew of Osbert and Edith, tells this story of a youthful encounter with the Countess, who was a highly experienced and somewhat world-weary woman. At the age of 19, and having just left Eton, Reresby plucked up the courage to ask Idina out for the evening and to his great surprise she accepted. Because his experience of life was rather limited the conversation soon turned to life at school. Warming to his theme, Reresby confided to the Countess that he had hated Eton – the food, the lessons, the teachers, the other boys and, most of all, the beatings. At the mention of the last the Countess's eyes lit up and she purred: 'Dear boy. Such a shame you were too young to appreciate them!'

MRS J.D. FENNA

Youth is stranger than fiction.

DOROTHY FULDHEIM (b. 1893; American writer)

Youth is a disease from which we all recover.

MARGARET BLAIR JOHNSTONE

I'm starting to wonder what my folks were up to at my age that makes them so doggoned suspicious of me all the time.

FRAN LEBOWITZ (b. 1951; American writer)

Remember that as a teenager you are at the last stage in your life when you will be happy to hear that the phone is for you.

JENNIE LEE (b. 1904; Scottish politician)

Quoted by Jill Craigie in *The Times*, 12 November 1980, when they were discussing the emotional problems of a mutual friend):

The trouble is, Jane is still young enough to think one man may be better than another.

MARY WILSON LITTLE (19th c.; American writer)

A youth with his first cigar makes himself sick; a youth with his first girl makes other people sick.

NANCY MITFORD (1904–73; English novelist and biographer)

From *The Pursuit of Love*:

The high spirits which he had seemed to possess must have been due to youth, drink and good health. Now that he was grown up and married he put all three resolutely behind him.

DOROTHY PARKER (1893–1967; American writer, satirist and humorist)

People ought to be one of two things, young or old. No; what's the good of fooling? People ought to be one of two things, young or dead.

GERTRUDE STEIN (1874–1946; American writer)

From *The Autobiography of Alice B. Toklas*:

It was not long after that that everybody was twenty-six. During the next two or three years all the men were twenty-six years old. It was the right age apparently for that time and place . . . If they were young men they were twenty-six. Later on, much later on, they were twenty-one and twenty-two.

MME SWETCHINE (1782–1857; Russian writer)
Youth should be a savings-bank.

ZANY

ERMA BOMBECK (b. 1927; American writer and humorist)
On a particularly cloying television programme about family life:

I once bragged that I saved a diabetic's life by throwing my body in front of a *Donna Reed* re-run.

ELEANOR BRON (b. 1934; English actress)
From *The Pillow Book of Eleanor Bron*:

We were still fast asleep in my attic room on the second-hand sofa bed I had bought for £20 at Peckham Rye, when there was a ring at the front door, five floors down. It was repeated and this time prolonged. I jumped out of bed, intrigued to know who could be calling at such an unearthly hour – it was about 10.30 in the morning – and fearing the worst. From my tiny balcony I could just make out far below, the edge of a basket that looked familiar, and in it, the nodding heads of daffodils. Then a lean, tanned hand wearing a wedding ring was laid along the rim of the basket, fingers gently frumming. It was unmistakably my mother. I said, 'It's my mother.' Whereupon the half-slumbering soul on the bed leapt as though electrified and began to gibber, clambering into his shirt. 'For God's sake!' he hissed, struggling. 'My tie! My tie! Find my tie!' I found his tie but could not keep from pointing out to him that although my mother might indeed think it a little off to meet him like this without his tie, she was observant enough to notice, and still more likely to take amiss, the fact that he was as yet not wearing any trousers.

MRS PATRICK CAMPBELL (1865–1940; English actress)
Mrs Pat was devoted to her Pekingese, Pinkie Panky Poo, and was determined to take him on all her travels. Once she tried to

smuggle him past customs by wrapping him in the voluminous folds of her cloak.

'Everything was going splendidly,' she told friends later, 'until my bosom barked.'

PATRICIA COCKBURN (b. 1914; Irish travel writer)

On going to be presented at Court in the 1930s, from *Figure of Eight*:

My mother was annoyed because Daddy had announced earlier that as we should not get supper at Buckingham Palace until after the last debutante had been presented, he would get hungry – so he had bought sandwiches which, as he had nowhere else to put them, he had put in his bearskin helmet (never to be called a busby). Due to the heat, the lavish amount of butter in the sandwiches had melted, soaking his bearskin and was spreading everywhere. Mummy was terrified it would get on her, or on my dress. There she sat in her diamond tiara, trying to look calm and benign and muttering under her breath, 'Jack, Jack, how *could* you, I shall never forgive you.'

ANGIE DICKINSON (b. 1931; American actress)

In *The Mirror*, 1 October 1985:

So far I've always kept my diet secret but now I might as well tell everyone what it is . . . Lots of grapefruit throughout the day and plenty of virile young men.

In *The Mirror* the next day, Anne Robinson wrote:

Lots of grapefruit throughout the day and plenty of virile young men . . . But since her past escorts include Edward Kennedy, Frank Sinatra, Andy Williams and Julio Iglesias, I think the grapefruit deserves all the credit.

MARY DUNN (1900–58; English writer and social satirist, best known for her 'Lady Addle' books)

Some advice from Blanche, Lady Addle on coping with wartime food shortages (from *The World of Lady Addle*):

Puddings

I have always said that the menu is half the battle. Read that you are eating Zabaglione, and you will expect Zabaglione. That is why I stick to menus – in lovely silver holders – and that is why I was able proudly to announce on it the other day 'Banana Melba with whipped cream'. Let me tell you how it was done. For my banana, I cut out a turnip in *precisely* the same shape, covered it in custard, and made an exquisite 'top dressing' consisting of a pint of dried milk, sweetened with saccharine, to which I added a tube of one of the best and purest makes of tooth-paste, which whipped like a dream, and tasted faintly of peppermint, an added advantage as it disguised the fact that the turnip did not taste of banana. What could be simpler?

Which she follows by 'Make Do and Mend' advice:

Brighten up old buns by wrapping them in used flypapers and leaving in the sun for half an hour. They will be as shiny as the pre-war article – and a few flies will give the illusion of plentiful currants.

WHOOPI GOLDBERG (b. ?1949; American actress)

Playing a Jamaican woman in her one-woman show:

Now I tell you, this man, he ask me, come to the United States of America. He all wrinkled, I say, you look like de old *raisin*. He want me to clean and cook and have a little nooky . . . A while later now de old raisin come upstairs and he was naked and wrinkled wrinkled *wrinkled*, all I want to do is iron him.

SALLY JAMES (b. 1950; English TV presenter)

On childbirth:

Next time I'm not just having an epidural for the birth – I'm having one for the conception as well!

FLORENCE KING (b. 1936; American writer and critic)

From *Confessions of a Failed Southern Lady*:

I looked elsewhere and found the clitoris. I did not know it was a clitoris; I called it the 'bump'. As I studied it, the light dawned. This was the famous maidenhead. It had to be – it was the only thing I could find that looked like a head.

It was all clear now. Intercourse is when a man pressed on the bump until it falls off. When that happens, you aren't a virgin anymore.

There was only one thing that bothered me. What did you do with the bump after it fell off? Was there a Bump Fairy?

MAUREEN LIPMAN (b. 1946; English actress and writer)
From *How Was It For You?*:

The most important thing to remember about Shakespeare is that he was a writer, working on commission . . . I like to think that if the Bard were alive today he'd be out at the beach in Beverley Hills tapping out 'High Concept' Movies of the Week on his Wang Word Processor, up to his ruff in cocaine.

BETTE MIDLER (b. 1945; American actress, comedienne and singer)

I'm as confident as Cleopatra's pussy.

JOAN RIVERS (b. 1939; American comedienne)

Mick Jagger's still my favourite – those lips. I saw him suck an egg out of a chicken.

Diana Ross is like a piece of liquorice in shoes. She walks into a pool hall and they chalk her head.

SOMERVILLE AND ROSS (Edith Oenone Somerville, 1858–1949; Violet Martin Ross, 1862–1915; Irish writers)
From *Some Experiences of an Irish RM*:

'More rain coming,' said Mr Knox, rising composedly; 'you'll have to put a goose down these chimneys some day soon; it's the only way in the world to clean them.'

BIBLIOGRAPHY AND SUGGESTIONS
FOR FURTHER READING

Ellen Dorothy Abb, *What Fools We Women Be*, 1937.

Polly Adler, *A House Is Not A Home*, 1953.

Zoe Akins, *Daddy's Gone A-Hunting*, 1921.

Judy Allen, *Picking on Men*, Arrow 1985.

Cleveland Amory, *Who Killed Society?*, 1960.

Mark Amory (ed.), *The Letters of Ann Fleming*, Collins 1985.

Allen Andrews (comp.), *Quotations for Speakers and Writers*.

Minna Antrim, *Naked Truth and Veiled Allusions*, 1902.

Daisy Ashford, *The Young Visiters*, Chatto & Windus, 1984.

Nancy Astor, *My Two Countries*, 1923.

Jane Austen, *Emma*.
    Mansfield Park.
    Pride and Prejudice.
    Sense and Sensibility.

Mary Hunter Austin, *The Land of Little Rain*, 1903.

Pam Ayres, *All Pam's Poems*, Hutchinson, 1978.

Tallulah Bankhead, *Tallulah*, 1952.

Myrtie Lillian Barker, *I am Only One*, 1963.

Djuna Barnes, *Smoke and Other Early Stories*, Virago, 1985.

Margaret Ayer Barnes, *Years of Grace*, 1930.

Miriam Beard, *Realism in Romantic Japan*, 1930.

Helen Olcott Bell, *Letters & Social Aims: R.W. Emerson*, 1876.

Victoria Billings, *The Womansbook*, 1974.

Charlotte Bingham, *Coronet among the Weeds*, Heinemann, 1963.

Elena Petrovna Blavatsky, *Lucifer*, 1891.

Erma Bombeck, *Motherhood: The Second Oldest Profession*, Mcgraw Hill Inc and Macdonald & Co., 1983.

Catherine Bramwell-Booth with Ted Harrison, *Commissioner Catherine*, Darton, Longman & Todd Ltd, 1983.

Gyles Brandreth, *Great Sexual Disasters*, Crown Publishers Inc and Granada Publishing, 1984.

Denis Brian, *Tallulah Darling – A Biography of Tallulah Bankhead*, Macmillan New York, 1972.

Eleanor Bron, *The Pillow Book of Eleanor Bron*, Cape, 1985.

David Brown, *Star Billing: Tell-Tale Trivia from Hollywood*, Weidenfeld & Nicolson, 1985.

Dee Brown, *The Gentle Tamers: Women of the Old West*, Barrie & Jenkins, 1973.

Peter Harry Brown and Pamela Ann Brown, *The MGM Girls: Behind the Velvet Curtain*, Harrap 1984.

Elizabeth Barrett Browning, *Aurora Leigh*, 1856.

Martha Bensley Bruère-Mary Ritter Beard, *Laughing their Way*, Macmillan New York, 1934.

George Burns, *The Third Time Around*, G.P. Putnam's Sons and W.H. Allen, 1980.

Stephanie Calman, *Gentlemen Prefer My Sister*, Heinemann, 1984.

Celebrity Research Group, *The Bedside Book of Celebrity Gossip*, Crown Publishers, 1984.

Edna D. Cheney, *Louisa May Alcott: Her Life, Letters and Journal*, 1889.

Patricia Cockburn, *Figure of Eight*, Chatto & Windus, 1985.

Colette, *Break of Day*.

    Cheri.

    Gigi.

    Music Hall Sidelights.

    The Photographer's Missus.

Joan Collins, *Past Imperfect*, Simon & Schuster Inc and W.H. Allen & Co. Ltd., 1978.

John Robert Colombo (ed.), *The Wit and Wisdom of the Moviemakers*, Hamlyn.

Jilly Cooper, *Class*, Eyre Methuen, 1979.

    Super-Jilly, Eyre Methuen, 1977.

Jilly Cooper and Tom Hartman, *Violets & Vinegar*, Allen & Unwin, 1980.

Wendy Cope, *Making Cocoa for Kingsley Amis*, Faber & Faber, 1986.

Lore and Maurice Cowan, *The Wit of Medicine*, Leslie Frewin, 1972.

    The Wit of Women, Leslie Frewin, 1969.

Ross Cox, *Adventures on the Columbia River*.

Lillian Day, *Kiss and Tell*, 1931.

Shelagh Delaney, *A Taste of Honey*, 1959.

A Dictionary of Foreign Quotations.

Phyllis Diller, *The Joys of Aging and How to Avoid Them*, Doubleday, 1981.

Al Diorio, *Barbara Stanwyck*, W.H. Allen, 1984.

Robert E. Drennan, *The Algonquin Wits*, 1968.

Carol Ann Duffy, *Standing Female Nude*, Anvil, 1985.

Elaine Dundy, *The Dud Avocado*, Gollancz, 1958.

Mary Dunn, *The World of Lady Addle*, Methuen, 1936.

Kenneth Edwards, *I wish I'd said that!*, Abelard, 1976.

George Eells, *Hedda and Louella*, W.H. Allen, 1972.

George Eells and Stanley Musgrove, *Mae West: The lies, the legends, the truth*, Robson Books, 1981.

George Eliot, *Adam Bede*.
Daniel Deronda.
The Mill on the Floss.

Esar, *Treasury of Humorous Quotations*.

Clifton Fadiman, *The Book of Anecdotes*, Little, Brown Inc and Faber, 1985.

Edna Ferber, *Roast Beef Medium. The Business Affairs of Emma McChesney*.

Paul Ferris (ed.), *Dylan Thomas: The Collected Letters*, Macmillan New York and J.M. Dent & Sons Ltd, 1985.

Margaret Fishback, *The Lie of the Land*.

Roland Flamini, *Ava: A Biography*, Robert Hale, 1984.

Rachel Heyhoe Flint, *Heyhoe!*, Pelham Books, 1978.

Brian Forbes, *Ned's Girl, The Life of Edith Evans*, Little, Brown Inc and Elm Tree Books, 1977.

Helen Franks, *Prime Time*, Pan, 1981.

Michael Freedland, *Errol Flynn*, William Morrow & Co. Inc and Arthur Barker Ltd, 1978.
Fred Astaire, W.H. Allen, 1976.
James Cagney, W.H. Allen, 1974.
Sophie, Woburn Press, 1978.

Mavis Gallant, *A Fairly Good Time*, 1970.

Elizabeth Gaskell, *Cranford*.

Charles Neilson Gattey, *Great Dining Disasters*, Columbus Books, 1984.

Renie Gee (comp.), *Who Said That?*
Still More of Who Said That?

Robert Giddings, *Musical Quotes and Anecdotes*, Longman, 1984.

John Gielgud *Distinguished Company*, Heinemann, 1972.

Hermione Gingold, *The World is Square*, 1945.

A. Glyn, *Elinor Glyn*, Hutchinson, 1955.

Elinor Glyn, *The Vicissitudes of Evangeline*, Duckworth, 1905.

Sheilah Graham, *My Hollywood*, Michael Joseph, 1984.

Virginia Graham, *Say Please*.

Joyce Grenfell, *'Stately as a Galleon' and other Songs and Sketches*, Macmillan, 1978.
In Pleasant Places, 1979.

John Grigg, *Nancy Astor*, 1980.

Alec Guinness, *Blessings in Disguise*, Alfred Knopf Inc and Hamish Hamilton Ltd, 1985.

173

Marcel Haedrich, *Coco Chanel, Her Life, Her Secrets*, 1971.

Peter Haining, *Raquel Welch*, W.H. Allen, 1984.

Donald Hall (ed.), *The Oxford Book of American Literary Anecdotes*, OUP, 1981.

Margaret Halsey, *With Malice Towards Some*, 1939.

Cicely Hamilton, *Marriage as a Trade*, 1981.

Robert Hamilton and Dorothy Shields, *Dictionary of Canadian Quotations*, McClelland & Stewart.

Lynn Haney, *Naked at the Feast*, Robson Books, 1981.

Helene Hanff, *Q's Legacy*, André Deutsch, 1985.

Warren G. Harris, *Gable and Lombard*, 1974.

Jane Harrison, *Reminiscences of a Student's Life*, 1925.

Sarah Harrison, *Hot Breath*, Macdonald, 1985.

Selina Hastings, *Life of Nancy Mitford*, Hamish Hamilton, 1985.

Jock Haswell, *James II*, 1972.

Lillian Hellman, *The Little Foxes*.
    Watch on the Rhine, 1946.

Dorothy Herman, *With Malice Toward All – Quips, Lives and Loves of Some Celebrated Twentieth Century Wits*, G.P. Putnam's Sons, 1982.

Xaviera Hollander, with Robin Moore and Yvonne Dunleavy, *The Happy Hooker*, Warner, 1972.

Hedda Hopper, *From Under My Hat*, Doubleday, 1952.

Hoyt's New Cyclopedia of Practical Quotations.

Naomi Jacob, *Our Marie*, 1936.

Erica Jong, *Fear of Flying*, Holt, Rinehart & Winston Inc and Secker & Warburg Ltd, 1974.

John Keats, *You Might As Well Live: The Life and Times of Dorothy Parker*, Simon & Schuster, 1970.

Christine Keeler with Sandy Fawkes, *Nothing But . . .*, New English Library, 1983.

Jean Kerr, *Please Don't Eat the Daisies*, 1957.
    The Snake Has All the Lines, 1958.

Milo Keynes (ed.), *Lydia Lopokova*, Weidenfeld & Nicolson, 1983.

Florence King, *Confessions of a Failed Southern Lady*, Michael Joseph, 1985.

Mary H. Kingsley, *Travels in West Africa* (ed. Elspeth Huxley), The Folio Society, 1976.

Francine Klabsbrun (ed.), *The First Ms. Reader*, 1972.

Elsa Lanchester, *Elsa Lanchester Herself*, Michael Joseph, 1983.

Joseph P. Lash, *Eleanor: The Years Alone*, W.W. Norton & Co Inc, 1972.

Fran Lebowitz, *Metropolitan Life*, E.P. Dutton & Co. Inc and Sidgwick &

Jackson Ltd, 1979.

Social Studies, Random House Inc and Sidgwick & Jackson Ltd, 1983.

Isobel Lennart, *Funny Girl*, 1964.

Leonard Louis Levinson (coll.), *Bartlett's Unfamiliar Quotations*.

Alan Levy, *Forever Sophia*, Robert Hale, 1980.

Beatrice Lillie, *Every Other Inch a Lady*, 1927.

Maureen Lipman, *How Was It For You?*, Robson Books, 1985.

Belle Livingstone, *Belle of Bohemia*, 1927.

Belle Out of Order, 1939.

Liz Lochhead, *True Confessions & New Clichés*, Polygon, 1985.

Christopher Logue (ed.), *Sweet & Sour, An Anthology of Comic Verse*, B.T. Batsford Ltd, 1983.

Anita Loos, *Gentlemen Prefer Blondes*, Liveright, 1925.

Fate Keeps on Happening, Harrap, 1985.

Shirley Lowe and Angela Ince, *Losing Control*, Macdonald, 1986.

Percy Lubbock, *Portrait of Edith Wharton*, 1947.

Phyllis McGinley, *A Pocketful of Rye*.

The Province of the Heart.

Ruth McKenney, *Guinea Pig*, Rupert Hart-Davis Ltd, 1938.

Shirley MacLaine, *Out On A Limb*, Bantam Books Inc and Elm Tree Books, 1983.

Macmillan Treasury of Relevant Quotations.

Victor Mallet (ed.), *Life with Queen Victoria*, John Murray, 1968.

Irving Mansfield, *Life with Jackie*, 1984.

Anthony Masters, *Nancy Astor, A Life*, McGraw Hill Inc and Weidenfeld & Nicolson Ltd, 1981.

Bette Midler, *A View from A Broad*, Simon & Schuster Inc. and Angus & Robertson, 1980.

Agnes de Mille, *Dance to the Piper*, 1952.

Alice Duer Miller, *Forsaking All Others*, 1931.

Casey Miller and Kate Swift, *Words and Women*, Gollancz, 1977.

Russell Miller, *The House of Getty*, Michael Joseph and Henry Holt & Co. Inc, 1985.

Margaret Mitchell, *Gone With the Wind*, 1936.

Jessica Mitford, *The American Way of Death*, Simon & Schuster and Hutchinson, 1978.

Hons and Rebels, 1960.

Lady Mary Wortley Montagu, *Essays and Poems* (eds R. Halsband and I. Grundy), OUP, 1977.

Joe Morella and Edward Z. Elstein, *Lana*, Citadel Press and W.H. Allen, 1972.

Fidelis Morgan, *The Female Wits, Women Playwrights of the Restoration*, Virago, 1981.

Margaret Morley, *Larger Than Life; the Biography of Robert Morley*, Robson Books, 1979.

Robert Morley, *Book of Bricks*, Weidenfeld & Nicolson.

Sheridan Morley, *Gertrude Lawrence*, Weidenfeld & Nicolson, 1981.
Gladys Cooper, Heinemann, 1979.
Marlene Dietrich, Elm Tree Books/Hamish Hamilton, 1979.

Jan Morris, *The Oxford Book of Oxford*, OUP, 1978.

Ann Morrow, *The Queen*, Granada, 1983.

Malcolm Muggeridge, *The Sun Never Sets*, Random House, 1940.

Frank Muir, *A Book at Bathtime*, Heinemann.
The Second Frank Muir Goes Into, Robson Books.

Dervla Murphy, *Full Tilt*, Century, 1983.

George Jean Nathan, *The Theatre in the Fifties*, 1953.

Margaret Nicholas (ed.), *The World's Greatest Lovers*, Octopus, 1985.

Anais Nin, *Winter of Artifice*, 1945.

Kathleen Norris, *Mother*, 1911.

Edna O'Brien *The Country Girls*, 1960.

Laura Pank (ed.), *Women's Words – The Dorma Book of Bedside Reading*, Elm Tree Books.

The Collected Dorothy Parker, Duckworth & Co. Ltd, 1973.

Molly Parkin, *Good Golly Ms Molly*, Star, 1978.
A Bit Between the Teeth, Ward Lock, 1985.

Laurence Peter, *Quotations For Our Time*, Bantam Books and Magnum, 1981.
Peter's Quotations, William Morrow, 1977.

Margot Peters, *Mrs Pat, The Life of Mrs Patrick Campbell*, The Bodley Head Ltd, 1984.

Virgilia Peters, *A Matter of LIfe and Death*, 1961.

Roy Plomley, *Plomley's Pick of Desert Island Discs*, Weidenfeld & Nicolson, 1982.

Mary Pettibone Poole, *A Glass Eye at the Keyhole*.

Ivy Baker Priest, *Green Grows Ivy*, 1958.

Susan Raven and Alison Weir, *Women in History*, Weidenfeld & Nicolson, 1981.

Jean Rhys, *Good Morning, Midnight*, André Deutsch, 1967.

Mary Roberts Rinehart, *Affinities and Other Stories*, 1920.

Mirian Ringo, *Nobody Said It Better!* Rand McNally & Co., 1980.

Joan Rivers, *The Life and Hard Times of Heidi Abromowitz*, Doubleday and

Comet, 1985.

Gwen Robyns, *Princess Grace*, W.H. Allen, 1976.

Michael Rogers, *Political Quotes*.

Kenneth Rose, *Kings, Queens and Courtiers*, Weidenfeld & Nicolson, 1985.

Helen Rowland, *A Guide to Men*, Dodge Publishing Co., 1922.
Personally Speaking.
Reflections of a Bachelor Girl.
The Rubaiyat of a Bachelor.

Audrey Russell, *A Certain Voice*, Ross Anderson Publications, 1984.

G.W.E. Russell, *Collections and Recollections*.

Adela Rogers Saint Johns, *Some Are Born Great*, 1974.

Anthony and Sally Sampson (eds), *Oxford Book of Ages*, OUP, 1985.

Olive Schreiner, *The Story of an African Farm*, 1985.

Florida Scott-Maxwell, *The Measure of My Days*, 1972.

Merle Shain, *Some Men are more perfect than Others*, 1973.

Nat Shapiro (ed.), *An Encyclopedia of Quotations about Music*, David & Charles, 1978.

Agnes Smedley, *Battle Hymn of China*, 1943.

Ella Smith, *Starring Miss Barbara Stanwyck*, 1974.

Stevie Smith, *The Collected Poems of Stevie Smith*, Allen Lane, 1975.

Gordon Snell, *The Book of Theatre Quotes*, Angus & Robertson, 1982.

Anne Somerset, *Ladies-in-Waiting*, Weidenfeld & Nicolson, 1984.

Somerville and Ross, *Some Experiences of an Irish RM*, J.M. Dent & Sons Ltd.

Sally Stanford, *The Lady of the House*, 1966.

Gertrude Stein, *QED*, 1903.
The Autobiography of Alice B. Toklas, 1933.
Everybody's Autobiography, 1937.

Gloria Steinem, *Outrageous Acts and Everyday Rebellions*, Cape, 1984.

Stewart, *A Dictionary of Political Quotations*.

Anthony Summers, *Goddess; The Secret Lives of Marilyn Monroe*, Macmillan New York and Gollancz, 1985.

Adam Sykes and Iain Sproat, *The Wit of Westminster*, Leslie Frewin 1972.

Irene Thomas, *The Bandsman's Daughter*, Macmillan, 1979.

Alice B. Toklas, *The Alice B. Toklas Cook Book*, 1954.

Rhoda Thomas Tripp, *The International Thesaurus of Quotations*, Penguin, 1976.

Jill Tweedie, *Letters from a Fainthearted Feminist*, Robson Books, 1982.
More from Martha: Further Letters from a Fainthearted Feminist, Robson Books, 1983.

Michelene Wandor, *Guests in the Body*, Virago, 1986.

Bill Wannan, *With Malice Aforethought*, Lansdowne Press, 1973.

Allen Warren, *Confessions of a Society Photographer*, Jupiter Books 1976.

P.G. Wells, *H.G. Wells in Love*, Faber. 1984.

Eudora Welty, *The Optimist's Daughter*, Random House Inc., 1969.

Mae West co-wrote and co-produced many of her films some of which are: *She Done Him Wrong (1933)*, *I'm No Angel (1933)*, *Belle of the Nineties* (1934), *Every Day's a Holiday* (1937).

Rebecca West, *The Abiding Vision*, 1935.

Katharine Whitehorn, *View from a Column*, Eyre Methuen, 1981. *Sunday Best*, Eyre Methuen. 1976.

Lady Wilson, *Letters from India*, Century-Hutchinson, 1984.

Robert Windeler, *Julie Andrews*, W. H. Allen. 1970.

Mary Day Winn, *Adam's Rib*, 1931.

Victoria Wood, *Up to you, Porky*, Methuen, 1985.

Marjorie Worthington, *Miss Alcott of Concord: A Biography*, Doubleday & Co., 1958.

Donald Zec and Anthony Fowles, *Barbra*, New English Library, 1981.

Philip Ziegler, *Diana Cooper*, Hamish Hamilton, 1981.

BIOGRAPHICAL INDEX

179

BARKER, Myrtie Lillian
Gossip

BARNES, Binnie
Pessimism

BARNES, Djuna
Death; Pessimism;
Understatement

BARNES, Margaret Ayer
Snobbery

BARR, Amelia
Marriage

BARRYMORE, Ethel
Acting; Insults

BASHKIRTSEFF, Marie
Women

BAUM, Vicki
Hollywood

BAXTER, Mrs G.
Children

BAYLIS, Lilian
Life; Quick Thinking; Youth

BEACHAM, Stephanie
Marriage

BEARD, Miriam
Snobbery

DE BEAUVOIR, Simone
Husbands

BEETON, Isabella
Food

BEHN, Aphra
Conversation

BELL, Helen Olcott
Religion

BENNETT, Constance
Hollywood

BERGEN, Candice
Hollywood

BERGMAN, Ingrid
Happiness

BERNHARDT, Sarah
Bitchery; Children; Fame;
Insults; Naivety; Pessimism

DE BERRI, Caroline, Duchesse
Adultery

BILLINGS, Victoria
Careers

BINGHAM, Charlotte
Clothes; Men; Pessimism;
Ridicule

BINGHAM, Madeleine
Food

BLAVATSKY, Helena
Travel

BLESSINGTON, Marguerite,
Countess of
Conversation; Love; Royalty

BLWEIN, Naomi
Men

BOEHM, Helen
Women

BOMBECK, Erma
Age; Children; Clothes;
Exercise; Food; Innuendo;
Marriage; Medicine; Zany

BOWEN, Elizabeth
Philosophy

BRACKEN, Peg
Money

BRAHMS, Caryl
Arts; War; Women;
Xenophobia

Clothes, Love; Ridicule;
Snobbery; Vanity;
Xenophobia

CONRAN, Shirley
Life

COOPER, Lady Diana
Age; Pessimism; Religion

COOPER, Dame Gladys
Acting; Quick Thinking;
Success; Understatement

COOPER, Jilly
Children; Literature; Sex;
Snobbery

COPE, Wendy
Conversation

CORELLI, Marie
Marriage

CORNUEL, Mme A.M. Bigot de
Life

COWAN, Annabel
Literature

CUNARD, Lady Emerald,
Naivety

DANIELS, Pauline
Jokes; Optimism

DAVIES, Marion
Innuendo

DAVIS, Bette
Arts; Careers; Death;
Marriage; Movies

DAY, Lillian
Snobbery

DU DEFFAND, Marie Anne,
Marquise
Religion

DEJAZET, Virginie

Xenophobia

DELANEY, Shelagh
Optimism

DENCH, Judi
Acting

DICKINSON, Angie
Zany

DIETRICH, Marlene
Love; Movies

DILLER, Phyllis
Age; Children; Exercise; Love;
Medicine; Men; Optimism;
Pessimism; Religion; Sex;
Vanity; Youth

DIX, Dorothy
Kindness

DOCKER, Lady
Xenophobia.

DORS, Diana
Quick Thinking

DOUGLAS, Sarah
Acting

DOWN, Lesley-Anne
Men

DUFFY, Carol Ann
Love

DUNN, Mary
Conversation; Vanity; Zany

DUNDY, Elaine
Naivety

EBNER-ESCHENBACH, Baroness
Marie von
Love

EDEN, Lady Clarissa, Countess of
Avon

Politics

EDGEWORTH, Maria
  Conversation; Gossip; Life

EKLAND, Britt
  Money

ELIOT, George
  Gossip; Jokes; Life; Men;
  Snobbery; Vanity; Women

QUEEN ELIZABETH I
  Royalty; War

QUEEN ELIZABETH II
  Marriage; Quick Thinking;
  Royalty; Understatement

QUEEN ELIZABETH THE
QUEEN MOTHER
  Families; Medicine; Royalty;
  Travel

EPHRON, Nora
  Children

ERROLL Idina, Countess of
  Youth

EVANS, Dame Edith
  Acting; Naivety; Religion;
  Snobbery; Success

FASCINATING AIDA (Dillie
  Keane; Marilyn Cutts; Adele
  Anderson)
  Snobbery

FENNA, Mrs J.D.
  Youth

FERBER, Edna
  Movies; Philosophy; Sex

FISHBACK, Margaret
  Appearance

FLEMING, Ann
  Divorce; Insults; Marriage;

Pessimism

FLINT, Rachel Heyhoe
  Exercise; Innuendo,
  Pessimism;

FONDA, Jane
  Movies

FONTEYN, Dame Margot
  Arts

FRANCIS, Connie
  Naivety

FROST, Lady Carina
  Vanity

FULDHEIM, Dorothy
  Youth

FULLER, Margaret
  Ridicule

FULLERTON, Fiona
  Xenophobia

GABOR, Zsa Zsa
  Adultery; Age; Divorce;
  Families; Husbands; Love;
  Marriage; Men; Naivety; Sex

GALLANT, Mavis
  Clothes

GARBO, Greta
  Exercise

GARDEN, Mary
  Quick Thinking

GARDNER, Ava
  Ridicule

GARDNER, Isabella Stewart
  Snobbery

GARLAND, Judy
  Marriage; Understatement

GARSON, Greer

Bitchery

GASCOIGNE, Jill
   Age

GASKELL, Elizabeth
   Kindness; Philosophy

GELLHORN, Martha
   Ridicule

GIBBS, Willa
   Religion

GILMAN, Charlotte Perkins
   Stetson
   Marriage; Vanity

GINGOLD, Hermione
   Acting; Careers; Politics;
   Xenophobia

DE GIRARDIN, Delphine
   Money

GISH, Dorothy
   Hollywood

GLASGOW, Ellen
   Marriage; Philosophy

GLYN, Elinor
   Adultery; Life; Sex

GODDARD, Paulette
   Happiness; Quick Thinking

GOLDBERG, Whoopi
   Zany

GORDON, Ruth
   Life; Quick Thinking

PRINCESS GRACE OF MONACO
   Understatement

GRAHAM, Virginia
   Exercise; War

GRAMAN, Jean
   Success

GREEN, Hetty
   Money

GREER, Germaine
   Sex

GRENFELL, Joyce
   Insults; Snobbery; Women

GREVILLE, The Hon. Mrs Ronald
   Philosophy

GREY, Mrs Harrington
   Snobbery

GUILFOYLE, Agnes
   Guilt

GUINAN, Texas
   Adultery; Appearance; Death;
   Fame; Food; Hollywood;
   Husbands; Love; Marriage;
   Movies; Politics; Ridicule

GWYNN(E), Nell
   Innuendo; Money; Quick
   Thinking

HALL, Jerry
   Life

HALSEY, Margaret
   Appearance; Clothes;
   Conversation; Xenophobia

HANDL, Irene
   Hollywood

HANFF, Helene
   Literature; Medicine

HARPER, Lucille S.
   Understatement

HARRIMAN, Margaret Case
   Money

HARRISON, Sarah
   Sex

HAYES, Helen

Marriage; Medicine; Men;
Understatement

KHASHOGGI, Soraya
Divorce

KING, Florence
Food; Literature; Marriage;
Pessimism; Religion; Zany

KINGSLEY, Mary
Travel

KINSEY, Mrs Alfred
Sex

KIRK, Lisa
Conversation

LAMARR, Hedy
Success

LAMPORT, Felicia
Pessimism

LANCHESTER, Elsa
Bitchery; Vanity

LANE, Ellie
Jokes

LARAMORE, Vivian Yeiser
Kindness

LAWRENCE, Gertrude
Money

LAYE, Evelyn
Sex

LEAR, Amanda
Gossip

LEBOWITZ, Fran
Conversation; Food; Guilt;
Success; Xenophobia; Youth

LEE, Emma
Women

LEE, Gypsy Rose

Arts

LEE, Jennie
Youth

LEE, Peggy
Movies

LEHMANN, Rosamond
Insults

LEJEUNE, Caroline
Movies

DE LENCLOS, Ninon
Age

LENNART, Isobel
Life

LEWIS, Rosa
Snobbery

LILLIE, Beatrice
Arts; Families; Quick
Thinking

LIPMAN, Maureen
Arts; Careers; Exercise; Jokes;
Medicine; Sex; Success; Zany

LITTLE, Mary Wilson
Age; Death; Divorce; Success;
Youth

LIVINGSTONE, Belle
Appearance; Careers; Death;
Food; Guilt

LLOYD, Marie
Food; Life; Snobbery;
Understatement; Vanity

LOCHHEAD, Liz
Exercise; Gossip;

LOMBARD, Carole
Husbands; Marriage; Women

LONGWORTH, Alice Roosevelt
Bitchery; Families; Gossip;

Insults; Kindness; Medicine;
Philosophy; Politics; Ridicule;
Sex

LOOS, Anita
Appearance, Hollywood;
Husbands; Insults; Literature;
Quick Thinking

LOPOKOVA, Lydia
Age; Conversation; Families;
Happiness; Innuendo; Men;
Optimism; Sex; Xenophobia

LOREN, Sophia
Marriage

LOTNEY, Emily
Food

PRINCESS LOUISE (Caroline
Alberta)
Understatement

LOWE, Shirley
Food

LOWELL, Amy
Happiness; Pessimsim

LOY, Myrna
Life; Movies

LUCE, Clare Boothe
Divorce; Fame; Marriage;
Politics; Women

LUMLEY, Joanna
Literature

LUXEMBURG, Rosa
Politics

DE LUYNES, Duchess
Religion

MABLEY, Moms
Innuendo

MACAULAY (Dame Emilie) Rose

Xenophobia

MCCOY, Mary
Money

MCGINLEY, Phyllis
Happiness; Optimism;
Philosophy; Politics

MCKENNEY, Ruth
Exercise

MCKINNEY, Joyce
Love

MACLAINE, Shirley
Careers; Money

MCLEOD, Lady Veronica
Snobbery

MACNAMARA, Caitlin
Ridicule

DE MAINTENON, Marquise
Success

MANNES, Marya
Sex

MANSFIELD, Jayne
Marriage; Men

HER ROYAL HIGHNESS THE
PRINCESS MARGARET
Death; Travel

MARGOLYES, Miriam
Religion

MARION, Frances
Movies

MARSH, Mary
Age

QUEEN MARY
Arts; Understatement; War

MAY, Elaine
Guilt; Hollywood

MEADE, Mrs H.
  Families
MEIR, Golda
  Politics
MELBA, Dame Nellie
  Vanity; Xenophobia
MENKEN, Adah Isaacs
  Optimism
MERMAN, Ethel
  Acting
METTERNICH, Fürstin Princess
Paulina
  Sex
MEUX, Lady (née Mildred Sturt)
  Arts
MIDLER, Bette
  Hollywood; Jokes;
  Philosophy; Royalty; Sex;
  Travel; Xenophobia; Zany
MILLAY, Edna St Vincent
  Innuendo; Life
DE MILLE, Agnes
  Fame; Women
MILLER, Alice Duer
  Women
MISTINGUETT
  Sex
MITCHELL, Margaret
  Life
MITFORD, Jessica
  Death; Xenophobia
MITFORD, Nancy
  Literature; Snobbery; War;
  Youth
MONROE, Marilyn
  Quick Thinking; Success;

  Vanity
MONTAGU, Elizabeth
  Gossip; Success
MONTAGU, Lady Mary Wortley
  Insults; Marriage; Women
MOORE, Lorrie
  Adultery
MORE, Hannah
  Arts; Snobbery
MUGGERIDGE, Kitty
  Ridicule
MUMFORD, Ethel Watts
  Families; Life; Money
MURPHY, Dervla
  Travel

NEVILLE, Lady Dorothy
  Conversation
NIGHTINGALE, Florence
  Life; Philosophy
NIN, Anaïs
  Appearance;

O'BRIEN, Edna
  Appearance; Naivety
OLIPHANT, Margaret
  Vanity
OLIVER, Anne
  Snobbery
ONO, Yoko
  Ridicule
OSTMAN, Virginia
  Careers

PAGE, La Wanda
  Insults
PAGET, Lady Victor

Snobbery

PARKER, Dorothy
Acting; Adultery; Appearance;
Bitchery; Careers; Children;
Clothes; Conversation; Death;
Divorce; Food; Gossip; Guilt;
Innuendo; Insults; Kindness;
Life; Literature; Love;
Marriage; Medicine; Men;
Money; Movies; Optimism;
Pessimism; Quick Thinking;
Ridicule; Sex; Snobbery;
Youth

PARKIN, Molly
Marriage; Philosophy

PARSONS, Louella
Hollywood

PEARL, Cora
Ridicule

PEARSON, Maryon
Success

PETER, Irene
Life

PETERSON, Virgilia
Politics

PFIZER, Beryl
Clothes; Families

PHIPPS, Mrs Paul
Royalty

PICON, Molly
Optimism

POGREBIN, Letty Cottin
Pessimism

DE POITIERS, Diane, Duchesse
de Valentinois
Gossip; Philosophy

DE POMPADOUR, Marquise

Jeanne Antoinette
Vanity

POOLE, Mary Pettibone
Snobbery

POTOR, Aurelia
Appearance

PRIEST, Ivy Baker
Money

REDESDALE, Lady
Naivety

REPPLIER, Agnes
Gossip

RHYS, Jean
Death

RIDING, Laura
Religion

RINEHART, Mary Roberts
Children

RIVERS, Joan
Age; Appearance; Bitchery;
Children; Clothes; Exercise;
Families; Guilt; Husbands;
Innuendo; Insults; Kindness;
Medicine; Men; Naivety;
Pessimism; Ridicule; Royalty;
Sex; Success; Travel; Vanity;
Zany

ROBINSON, Anne
Zany

ROOSEVELT, Eleanor
Politics

ROS, Amanda McKitterick
Literature

ROWLAND, Helen
Adultery; Appearance;
Divorce; Husbands; Marriage;
Men; Pessimism

RUCKELSHAUS, Jill
   Women

VAN RUNKLE, Theadora
   Death

RUSSELL, Jane
   Fame

RUSSELL, Rosalind
   Life

SAGAN, Françoise
   Men

SAINT JOHNS, Adela Rogers
   Husbands; Politics; Sex;
   Success; Women

SAND, George
   Vanity

SCHENLEY, Ruth S.
   Food

SCHREINER, Olive
   Women

SCOTT-MAXWELL, Florida
   Children

SCULL, Mrs Barclay
   Snobbery

SEDLEY, Catharine, Countess of
Dorchester
   Ridicule

SERWAT, Mrs Henry J.
   Careers

DE SEVIGNÉ, Marie de Rabutin-
Chantal
   Men

SHAIN, Merle
   Adultery

SHIELDS, Brooke
   Naivety

SHRIVER, Pam
   Exercise

SHROEDER, Pat
   Politics

SIDDONS, Sarah
   Love

SIEFF, Louise
   Quick Thinking

SIMMONS, Mrs A.
   Life

SITWELL, Dame Edith
   Insults; Literature; Medicine;
   Snobbery; Vanity

SKINNER, Cornelia Otis
   Insults; Women

SMEDLEY, Agnes
   Understatement

SMITH, Stevie
   Philosophy; Royalty

SOMERVILLE AND ROSS (Edith
Oenone Somerville and Violet
Martin Ross)
   Zany

SPALDING, Elizabeth W.
   Life

SPARK, Muriel
   Snobbery

SPENCER, Raine, Countess,
   Snobbery

STANFORD, Sally
   Sex

STANTON, Elizabeth Cady
   Politics; Religion

STANWYCK, Barbara
   Divorce; Hollywood; Movies

WELLS, Carolyn
Divorce; Guilt; Money;
Vanity; Women

WEST, Mae
Acting; Arts; Bitchery;
Careers; Conversation;
Exercise; Food; Innuendo;
Insults; Jokes; Kindness; Life;
Marriage; Medicine; Men;
Money; Naivety; Optimism;
Philosophy; Politics; Quick
Thinking; Religion; Ridicule;
Sex; Sport; Success;
Understatement; Vanity

WEST, Dame Rebecca
Age; Arts; Innuendo; Money;
Politics; War

WHARTON, Edith Newbold
Quick Thinking

WHITEHORN, Katharine
Families; Guilt; Jokes;
Marriage; Women

WHITTON, Charlotte
Success

WILCOX, Ella Wheeler
Gossip

WILLIAMS, Esther
Movies

WILLIAMS, Shirley
Politics

WILSON, Lady Anne
Gossip; Snobbery

WILSON, Lady Mary
Pessimism

WILSON, Mrs Woodrow
Marriage

WINN, Mary Day
Sex

WINSLOW, Thyra Samter
Love

WINTERS, Shelley
Clothes; Vanity

DE WOLF, Elsie
Travel

WOOD, Peggy
Insults

WOOD, Victoria
Children; Food; Life

WOODVILLE, Lady Elizabeth
Adultery

WOOLF, Virginia
Literature; Snobbery

WYMORE, Patrice
Bitchery

YATES, Paula
Jokes

ACKOWLEDGEMENTS

The extracts listed below are reprinted with kind permission of the following:

W.H. Allen Ltd: George Eells, *Hedda and Louella*; Molly Parkin, *Good Golly Ms Molly*; and Joan Rivers, *The Life and Hard Times of Heidi Abromowitz*; Mark Amory and Mark Boxer, executors: *The Letters of Ann Fleming* (Collins Harvill); The Bodley Head and Alfred A. Knopf, Inc.: Margot Peters, *The Life of Mrs Patrick Campbell*, © Margot Peters; Chatto & Windus Ltd: Patricia Cockburn, *Figure of Eight*; Jonathan Cape Ltd and Henry Holt & Co. Inc.: Gloria Steinem, *Outrageous Acts and Everyday Rebellions*; Jonathan Cape Ltd and Richard Scott-Simon Ltd: Eleanor Bron, *The Pillow Book*; Robin Clark: Mary Dunn, The World of Lady Addle (Quartet Books Ltd): André Deutsch Ltd: Jean Rhys, *Good Morning Midnight*; Doubleday & Co. Inc.: © Phyllis Diller, 1981, *The Joys of Aging and How to Avoid Them*; Gerald Duckworth & Co.: Dorothy Parker, *The Collected Dorothy Parker*; Carol Ann Duffy: 'The Businessman's Love Poem', (Anvil Press); Faber & Faber Ltd: Wendy Cope, 'From June to December', published in *Making Cocoa for Kingsley Amis*; Victor Gollancz Ltd and Curtis Brown: Jessica Mitford, *Hons and Rebels*; *The Guardian*: items by Nancy Banks-Smith; Robert Hale Ltd: Janice James, 'The Bottom Line', published in *A Woman's Own World*; Hamish Hamilton Ltd: Philip Ziegler, *Diana Cooper*; A.M. Heath & Co.: Jessica Mitford, *The American Way of Death*; William Heinemann Ltd: Charlotte Bingham, *Coronet among the Weeds*; Heinemann Educational Books Ltd: John Gielgud, *Distinguished Company*; ICM, New York: Elaine Dundy, *The Dud Avocado*; Michael Joseph Ltd: Florence King, *Confessions of a Failed Southern Lady*, (US, St Martins Press); Macdonald & Co. Ltd: Erma Bombeck, *Motherhood, The Second Oldest Profession*; and Shirley Lowe and Angela Ince, *Losing Control*; James MacGibbon, executor: Stevie Smith, 'On the Death of a German Philosopher', published in *The Collected Poems of Stevie Smith* (Penguin Modern Classics); Macmillan Ltd: Joyce Grenfell, 'Stately as a Galleon' and Other Songs and Sketches; and Irene Thomas, *The Bandsman's Daughter*; Methuen & Co Ltd London: Jilly Cooper, *Class* and *Super Jilly*; and from Victoria Wood, *Up to You, Porky* (US, Richard Stone Artistes Presentation); John Murray Ltd: Dervla Murphy, *Full Tilt* (US, Overlook Press); W.W. Norton & Co: Anita Loos, *Gentleman Prefer Blondes*; Deborah Owen Ltd: Naomi Jacob, *Our Marie*; *The Observer*: Katharine Whitehorn, 'Mother'; Penguin Books Ltd: Gertrude Stein, *The Autobiography of Alice B. Toklas*; A.D.

Acknowledgements

Peters Ltd: Russell Miller, *The House of Getty*; Polygon, Edinburgh University Students Publication Board: Liz Lochead, verses published in *True Confessions & New Clichés*; Robson Books Ltd: Maureen Lipman, *How Was It For You?*; and Jill Tweedie, *Letters from a Fainthearted Feminist*; Dudley Russell: *Poems*, © Pam Ayres; Sidgwick & Jackson Ltd: Fran Lebowitz, *Metropolitan Life* (US, ICM, New York) and *Social Studies* (US, William Morris, New York); Simon & Schuster, Inc.: Margaret Halsey, *With Malice Towards Some*; *The Spectator*: Valerie Grove; Sun & Moon Press, Maryland: Djuna Barnes, *Smoke . . .* ; Virago Press Ltd: Gertrude Stein, *Everybody's Autobiography*; George Weidenfeld & Nicolson Ltd: Edna O'Brien, *The Country Girls*.

We have used our best endeavours to trace all holders of copyright in those items that warranted permission to reproduce, but have been unable to locate a small number of such holders. We will be glad to hear from these copyright-owners.

(M.B. & A.O'C.)

194

A selection of humour titles available in paperback from Grafton Books

John Grant
The Depths of Cricket   £2.95 ☐

Sam Llewellyn
Yacky Dar Moy Bewty   £2.50 ☐

Neil Martin
A Devastatingly Brilliant Exposé of Almost Everything   £2.50 ☐

Gyles Brandreth
Great Sexual Disasters (illustrated)   £3.50 ☐

N Sayers and C Viney
The Bad News Zodiac   £1.95 ☐
The Bad News Horrorscope   £2.50 ☐

Ellis Weiner
National Lampoon's Doon   £2.50 ☐

To order direct from the publisher just tick the titles you want
and fill in the order form.   GF2481

Modern society – now available in Grafton Books

Dougal Dixon
After Man (illustrated)   £4.95   ☐

Germaine Greer
The Female Eunuch   £3.95   ☐

John Howard Griffin
Black Like Me   £1.95   ☐

Peter Laurie
Beneath the City Streets   £2.50   ☐

Desmond Morris
The Pocket Guide to Manwatching (illustrated)   £5.95   ☐
Manwatching (illustrated)   £8.95   ☐
The Naked Ape   £2.95   ☐
Intimate Behaviour   £2.95   ☐
The Human Zoo   £2.50   ☐
Animal Days (autobiography)   £1.95   ☐
Gestures (illustrated)   £3.95   ☐

José Silva and Michael Miele
The Silva Mind Control Method   £2.95   ☐

Ivan Tyrell
The Survival Option (illustrated)   £2.50   ☐

Michael Binyon
Life in Russia   £2.95   ☐

To order direct from the publisher just tick the titles you want
and fill in the order form.   **GM881**

All these books are available at your local bookshop or newsagent, or can be ordered direct from the publisher.

To order direct from the publishers just tick the titles you want and fill in the form below.

Name _____

Address _____

Send to:
Grafton Cash Sales
PO Box 11, Falmouth, Cornwall TR10 9EN.

Please enclose remittance to the value of the cover price plus:

UK 60p for the first book, 25p for the second book plus 15p per copy for each additional book ordered to a maximum charge of £1.90.

BFPO 60p for the first book, 25p for the second book plus 15p per copy for the next 7 books, thereafter 9p per book.

Overseas including Eire £1.25 for the first book, 75p for second book and 28p for each additional book.

Grafton Books reserve the right to show new retail prices on covers, which may differ from those previously advertised in the text or elsewhere.